FISHING FOR SALMON

Fishing for Salmon

Charles McLaren

JOHN DONALD PUBLISHERS LTD
EDINBURGH

To my wife
Barbara

© Charles McLaren 1977
All rights reserved.
Published by John Donald Publishers Ltd.,
8 Mayfield Terrace, Edinburgh EH9 1SA

Printed and bound in Great Britain by
Morrison & Gibb Ltd, London and Edinburgh

Preface

Is it the memory of the first salmon I caught on fly, before school one morning, when I was very small, young and alone; or, many years later, catching twelve in a few hours; or catching three in only four casts one evening; or, when fishing for seatrout meant not having certain flies on my cast, lest I hook a salmon? I do not know which moments I cherish most, but it may come to light as I write. No matter, so long as you sense some of the excitements I have had and find much in my ways and my thinking worth digesting.

Through planning, first by my father and then by myself, I have been privileged to do most of my fishing in fairly quiet waters. I was not born with a split-cane rod in my hand nor quiet water by my pram, and there was no good fishing laid on for me by chance of birth. But I have not had to move shoulder to shoulder on crowded rivers to do my fishing though I have experienced it and sympathise with those who have no other. I shall never fail to be grateful for my lot, yet my approach to fishing might not stand the strain of being on heavily hammered water for long.

Up to this time, 1977, I have caught 1936 salmon. My records are not complete and I have had to dig deep into my memory, but the calculation is carefully done and the figure reasonably accurate. It is not a phenomenal number and I recall the capture of most. These were caught on fly, and perhaps two hundred more spinning, trolling or on worm, excluding wartime 'landings'. They have come from a limited area — the rivers and lochs of Scotland and the Driva in Norway, which I fished for a week only. The length of experience in varied types of water may justify this attempt to share with others.

My study of fishing is based on teaching by my late father, a gamekeeper until he retired from it at forty-four, in 1920. He had a wide knowledge of fish and an uncanny ability to catch them. He made me well aware of the dangers of blindly following tradition and making the same old mistakes, year after year. I think his early use of hazel wands and horsehair, with a critical shortage of hooks, taught him much of a fundamental nature, which we do not pause to consider nowadays with all our modern aids — sadly so. I do not know that I accepted all his advice to begin with, at least not openly! I listened to it and watched with increasing care as the years went by, and I soon realised how wonderful it was to be able to work on the basis of all he had taught me.

I do not try, nor do I wish, to remove the mysteries of the sport, and I do not have the answers to all the questions. I cannot be certain how fish will react to my efforts, but I do say the uncertainties are not as great as many would have us believe, while admitting there are so many things we do not know about salmon. We all love fishing, however real or supposed the mystery which gives such joy and pleasure. It is a sport at which we can enjoy failure with honour.

There are many oft-heard sentiments which I dispute — 'The older one gets, the more one realises how little one knows about fishing' being one of them. 'Always' and 'Never' are words to be used with care, but I suggest, with respect, that many avoid them in relation to fishing because of their own lack of knowledge of principles. There are many basic rules in fishing and, until the angler is willing to accept this, he will remain less than a great fisherman. I think it is largely due to tradition that there is so much opposition to any form of dogmatism in relation to angling. There are many basic rights and wrongs and predictables in the sport, for example in casting or in 'striking' the fish. About a hundred years ago George M. Kelson wrote that, 'The drawing of false conclusions from just principles has been no less injurious to the unenlightened than the untold evil of drawing just conclusions from false principles'. I have heeded this well and I hope I shall justify my beliefs and give grounds for some dogmatism.

Only a controlled study of results can show where sound principles exist and where false theory and practice should be abandoned. In the absence of long and well-planned study, the art and science of salmon fishing remains controversial — so, surely, all fishers are entitled to their say!

Charles McLaren

Acknowledgements

I am greatly indebted to my lifelong friend R. Peter Clark of Aberdeen without whose help and encouragement this book would never have been written.

I am indebted also to Mr George Alden of Perth for permission to use his photographs and to The Scottish Tourist Board, Ravelston Terrace, Edinburgh for use of the colour transparency used in the cover design.

List of Photographs

Showing how to bring in a fish to net during an evening's instruction.

Start of a day from Culag Hotel, Lochinver.

Tackling up during morning's instruction by the river — ensuring rods properly assembled and knots well-tied.

Selection of fly is important — a bright fly or a dark one, and which size? The day's sport can depend on the right choice.

The author's daughters, Lorna and Barbara, started young and in difficult territory.

Note the 'black cap' of the kelt. A kelt must be returned to the water undamaged and it is important to hold it on an even keel head upstream until it is ready to swim off.

The author with two fine old ghillies, Peter Stewart and Hugh 'Begg' Sutherland, and a young one, Hugh's son Marcus, at Altnaharra.

Pointing out a good lie where two streams meet in the neck of the pool; a difficult return from the stance when a fish has been hooked.

The author fishing a good pool on the Kirkaig. The lies are on the far side of the stream at this height of water and casting is difficult.

Some casting successes in Scottish and British Casting Associations' Competitions.

A 'Steeple' or almost vertical back cast from a precarious stance: it is necessary to shoot line and the large fly required adds to the difficulties — The Kirkaig Falls Pool.

An awkward position high above the fish; they are difficult to hook from such a height and there is no lower stance.

A long cast, without apparent effort from the author, showing how the line is brought forward in a narrow loop.

Too high or too low water can make this stretch impassable by fish, but even at a suitable water level it is a rough run for them.

Jetties forming new lies where previously there was only shallow water, but often a new pool is made at the expense of the next pool downstream.

The result of a well-spent hour and a half on a favourite loch, fishing lies which had not been fished for many years.

Loch Naver — a delightful loch and one of Scotland's finest for salmon.

Contents

		Pages
Preface		v-vi
1.	The Salmon	1- 8
2.	Salmon in Rivers:	9-28
	Spring — Fishing the Pool — Backing — Running Fish — Patience — My First Salmon — Summer — Tackle — The Dropper and Three Flies — Autumn — Shade — The Short Rod — Light — A Perfect Day	
3.	Salmon in Lochs:	29-34
	Lies of Old — A Rod Reward for a Fish Caught — My Twelve Footer — The Short Rod Again	
4.	Striking Rises	35-39
5.	Playing a Fish	41-48
6.	Gaffing, Netting & Tailing Fish	49-54
7.	Wading	55-56
8.	Disturbance of Fish	57-59
9.	The Ghillie	61-66
10.	Other Than Fly	67-70
11.	Courtesies	71-74
12.	Intuition	75-78
13.	The Changing Scene	79-83
14.	Fishing Hotels	85-89
15.	A Caster's Angle	91-95
Index		97-99

1
The Salmon

The Salmon — the leaping fish — Salmo Salar as it was called by the Romans when they were here in the West and saw it in superabundance in the rivers; a leaping fish of silver, with body of sheer muscle.

Its life story is a fascinating one and its survival seems little short of miraculous; it is a scientific story, complex and still incomplete, told in a number of fine books but, very briefly, the tale of its life cycle is this.

In October and November, most male and female salmon, in pairs, reach the spawning redds in the tributaries and headwaters of the rivers, as well as in perhaps the whole length of the rivers themselves, even close to where they enter the sea. Frost at night encourages this movement.

The redds are of gravel and are scooped out by the female. She turns on her side and by movement of her tail sucks up gravel, which is carried down a few feet in the current, forming a depression and, below it, a heap of gravel through which the water flows. She works her way slowly upstream for possibly five or six feet, depositing the ova which are carried downstream into the gravel heap. The male moves in from time to time while shedding milt, which is carried down by the stream and fertilises the eggs. These may be as much as a foot deep in the gravel where they are usually assured of sufficient moisture for survival.

The hen fish seems to do all the work and the cock fish remains beside her or slightly behind. If he sees any intruding parr or other fish he chases it off viciously — a male parr can fertilise the eggs but it is not desirable.

A fair number of ova are not carried into the gravel but are

1

caught and held in the eddies, to be eaten up by parr and other small fish — 'rowan gatherers' as they are sometimes called; whitling also know of this source of food.

A great change in colour takes place before these fish reach the redds — the female, fat and rather unshapely, is dark on the back and greyish underneath, while the male, with his large, long head and a huge hook on the end of his lower jaw, has a tartan appearance — reds, pink, orange, brown and black. Both are well camouflaged and difficult to see — and not the beauties they used to be, when you do see them. A blink of sun can give the game away, but a real weakness in their defence is that their tails often show above water and there may be considerable splashing and movement. I watch almost every year and never cease to marvel at the origins and near end of what must surely be the king of all fish. All the mature fish do not die after spawning but most of them do; some may spawn five or six times and live for ten or more years.

A few apparently mature fish do not manage to spawn for some reason or other; they stay in the river with the kelts for a few months — silvery and in good condition to look at, but very poor to eat. If you hold such a fish up by the tail the spawn will move down towards the head and a bulge will show. These are known as Rawners or Baggit (Baggot) salmon.

After spawning they are spent fish — thin, weak and in poor condition, and known as kelts. The heavy floods of winter carry the weak away but the stronger ones stay in the lochs and rivers for three or four months. I suppose they may feed a little but it does not show, and they remain long and thin. The great change is that they become silvery again. The jaw hook of the male and all the colourings have gone. They are ready for their return to the sea, camouflaged for a few months' feeding before returning upstream to spawn again — or to be caught in a net or by a seal, or hooked by some crafty angler. They do not go far out to sea this time and they usually return to the stream they left, though a few have been known to stray up other rivers.

It would seem a good idea to get these kelts back to the sea and good feeding as soon as possible. An attempt to give a small number help in this way was made some years ago. The fish were trapped thirty miles or so from the sea at spawning time. They were stripped (artificially spawned), marked with a tag and taken down to the estuary, where they were released; within three days these fish were back in the traps in the river from which they were taken such a short time before — a thirty miles swim back upstream to try and get the ways of nature put to right again. It seems we may help nature along but not alter it. They were not ready to return to sea, physiologically unprepared to be in salt water and feed there.

Fishings open early and anglers are out with flies and baits searching for the treasured Spring Salmon while there are still many kelts in the rivers and lochs. Kelts must be returned to the water unharmed, and an angler may have difficulty in recognising one and distinguishing it from a fresh-run salmon. Some kelts seem in fair shape and good colour, while some clean fish only fair in shape and colour, as in the case of a fish returning to the river for the second time. It may seem easy here, while we sit in comfort, to picture a kelt but, when beside the river or in a boat, and perhaps a little cold and weary, wishful thinking, while viewing a catch, may turn concave contours into convex ones and silver may gleam unduly. Some kelts play well when hooked. If it is returned to the water who is the witness to the catch of even a kelt? And what if it is a good fish? There isn't much time to decide: kill a possible kelt, which will probably die anyway, or return a clean fish, maybe — the first 'take' of the year. A dreadful dilemma for the angler who does not see many fish, kelt or clean, and it is illegal to kill a kelt.

A number of distinguishing features should prevent mistakes. A good test is to lay the fish on a flat surface and look at its general outline. In a kelt the middle third of its body has almost parallel contours (that is, the dorsal and ventral contours), the back being very slightly convex. In a clean fish these contours are plainly convex, even if the fish is very thin. The thin fish with dark and tartan colourings gives no problems and is surely a kelt. The vent protrudes in the kelt, the tail and fins may be frayed, the head looks largish for the body and has a very distinctive black cap. The gills are pale, and there may be freshwater gill maggots on them. A clean-run fish which has spawned previously might also have these gill maggots, but its gills are red and healthy and its general condition is good in most cases. A fresh fish might have sealice on it, but not so a kelt, unless very close to brackish tidal water. When due to return to the sea the kelt is silvery with a dull, pearly-looking, silver. The silver of the fresh fish or 'clean' fish is bright, with perhaps a hint of pinkness and a greenish back.

The pundits produced a formula to calculate the condition of a salmon, where K is the coefficient of condition, W is the weight of the fish in pounds, and L is the length in inches from tip of snout to centre V of tail; then K equals W x 100,000 divided by L cubed x 36. When K is one or more the condition is good, but when ·8 or less the condition is poor and the fish is probably a kelt. There will hardly be time to do this sum when the fish has just been netted!

There is no knowing how many kelts survive after the further exertions involved in being caught but, if any do, and come back to the river, then it is worth returning them to the water carefully. Hold them on an even keel, with head into the stream until they swim away. I do not believe that to throw them spinning head over tail into river or loch is a good means of resuscitation. Nor should one play a fish lightly or easily in an effort to save its energies — this exhausts it completely. Better to get it in as quickly as possible.

I recall from many years ago, when I was running a large sporting hotel in the Highlands, a holiday angler among the guests sought me out quietly. When I went out, he had a rolled-up towel under his left arm. As I approached he glanced around the hall and, with his right hand, began to undo the end of the rolled towel. Raised eyebrows beckoned me over to bend down and peer into the opening. 'What is it?' he asked. 'A kelt,' I whispered. He nodded, closed the towel, and wheeled away in shame. No further reference was ever made to it. I wonder if he will read this and remember?

On another occasion — so different — three 'experienced' and very eager fishermen guests brought in a huge tray of fish. They celebrated their catch blissfully unaware that the fish were all large seatrout kelts. I could not close my eyes to this, but the anglers were most indignant. They departed next day and, happily, I have not seen them since. Such events are very damaging to our seatrout stocks: they spawn frequently and kelts are valuable but, alas, ignorance and greed deplete our stocks in many estuaries and rivers to this day. Usually we see kelts only in the Spring, perhaps until May, but in a drought year in the 'fifties I saw a seatrout kelt on 17th September. It had not been able to get out of the loch and down to the sea.

The adult fish are away, so what of the ova just spawned and left to face the future without parental care? The choice of redd was of vital importance. There are usually seven or eight hundred eggs per pound weight of the female fish so there are a great many of them but only about ·1% reach the salmon stage and return to the river.

These eggs remain in the redd during the incubation period, which is about three months, depending on the temperature of the water — low temperatures lengthening it. They survive being frozen, but damage to the redds and eggs is possible at the thaw when ice-flows break up and bruise the eggs or expose them to fish and fowl, always ready to enjoy such a succulent bite.

The eggs develop eyes and then hatch out into tiny fish, with a yolk sac beneath their bellies. This yolk sac provides nourishment for about six weeks, while they become able to fend for themselves. When I was running angling courses for the Scottish Council of Physical Recreation — some in the Spring each year — I used to have a dozen or so of these small fish, alevins, in a large glass jar so that they could be seen and watched at this stage. I selected some normal and some freaks, with two heads or other abnormalities. They all grew well to begin with, but became thinner as they needed more food and the sac became smaller. The freaks died, but the normal ones hunted for food as soon as they were released into the river; one, I remember vividly, swallowed a water mite and seemed to have a dreadful time overcoming it! It is vital that there should be ample food available as they lose their yolk sacs. Pollution from waste, and the choking of this food supply by fine peat deposits or the like, can take a heavy toll of these alevins. Damage by floods, ice and such forces of nature are usually overcome by nature, but man-made schemes such as water extraction, hydro schemes, drainage and overnetting have reduced our stocks. Although some of these schemes are essential for our welfare, common sense must be used in regulating our netting, disposal of waste, and so on. We tend to be a little selfish and greedy.

When the yolk sac has gone and the fish are really foraging for their own food they are called fry and are known as such until towards the end of the first summer — then they are known as parr and might be caught when fishing with worm or fly. The penalty for killing a parr is a fine of £5 — it should be more now. It is a valuable fish when a vast number of ova and alevins and fry have perished. The surviving parr is a beautiful little fish, just a few inches long, spotted like a small brown trout but with eight or so distinctive marks down each side of its body from head to tail, like fingertip marks. If you do catch one, take the hook out carefully and quickly, and return it to the water. The strong parr develops into a fine salmon, so its welfare is of great importance. The one which grows up fighting currents and foraging successfully for food does well in the sea, where food is abundant.

A parr may stay four or five years in fresh water but it is usually two years and four months or so old and five or six inches long when, towards the beginning of May, it becomes known as a smolt. Over a period of just a week or two, it develops a covering of temporary scales and becomes like a little bar of silver. The fins and tail grow well and it is ready to start the long swim in the seas. These scales will stick to your hand if you have the occasion to take hold of a smolt and the parr markings show again where bare of scales; the permanent scales become silvery later in the salt water. The smolts congregate in shoals as they go downstream and you can see them in great numbers in rivers, rising to flies; many are caught at this time by trout anglers and, as with parr, they must be put back. It is said the first spate in May takes the smolts away, and this is often true, but they will move down when they are good and ready, even in low water. A small spate is best of all for this migration to the sea as the silvery sheen is not good camouflage in fresh water.

Few ova, alevins, fry or parr survive to maturity under the ravages of dragonfly larvae, eels, waste, ice, flood and drought, and other predators among birds and fish and, alas, some anglers. A variety of hazards lie ahead in the ocean, on the journey out to the feeding grounds, and on the journey back up river to the spawning redds.

When they reach the sea the young salmon go far away to feed. The west coast of Greenland, the Faroes and Norway are among the vast feeding grounds where crustaceans, seafish fry and sprats abound.

Some stay in the sea feeding for only a year or so, through one winter, before returning to the rivers when they are known as grilse. This is a slender fish compared with a fully grown salmon, its body tapering to a very narrow 'wrist' above a deeply forked tail; this presents difficulty to some who would 'tail' one by hand rather than net it or gaff it. Experienced anglers have written that it is not possible to 'tail' a grilse by hand, or even with wire tailer, but I shall in a later chapter demonstrate that this is not so. A grilse will spawn and return to the sea as a kelt but does not go far out this time, returning to the river before winter — a 'second return' fish and still a grilse. There are often discussions, if not real arguments, about whether a fish caught is a grilse or a salmon. A grilse may range in weight from about two pounds even to fourteen pounds, and a salmon from about two and a half pounds to, well, seventy or eighty pounds or more, if account of some lost is taken! The only accurate method of telling is by a scale reading, which shows if the fish has been in the sea for one winter or more, when fine feeding leads to rapid growth. Scale reading is a skilled task best left to the experts. A grilse has been in the sea for only one winter. A salmon has spent more than one winter. The grilse may well have spawned more than once.

The remainder which stay at sea for two or more winters return to their home rivers as salmon. What a wonderful sense of taste or smell or homing instinct leads them there! It is surely said some fresh salmon return to the larger rivers every month of the year, perhaps only a few at times but each river has its own distinctive runs in Spring, Summer and Autumn. They have fed voraciously at sea, a reflex action, and a habit no doubt hard to break or control. Do we loosen control and trigger off this reflex action when we tempt them to feed in fresh water, where they do not normally feed? I shall think so until I am convinced otherwise.

The little smolts fight their way to the distant feeding grounds but many fall prey to the bigger sea fish, cormorants and others. A great toll is taken there by netsmen, when young and mature alike are taken indiscriminately — some thousands of tonnes each year. There are agreed restrictions on catches now and, with a declining salmon population, these restrictions must be carefully observed for conservation purposes. But how can they be enforced? Men may be too greedy and shortsighted for this. The lack of planning at some netting stations, and the lack of co-operation between them, the use of miles of nylon nets at sea by unauthorised fishers, support our worst fears. Disease also reduced stocks greatly. But restraint is perhaps too much to ask where salmon sells at such high prices.

Seals kill great numbers of fish, but otters, I think, do much more good than harm — they eat eels mainly, and the few salmon they do take are small 'rental' for their killing of eels. Anglers, fair and foul, do not make very great inroads into total stock, though they probably do to specific runs of fish, such as the Spring runs in some rivers.

The largest salmon caught in Scotland was one in the nets on the river Tay in 1872, and it weighed seventy pounds. The largest known was one of seventy-two pounds, caught on the river Tana in Norway in 1928. A sixty-seven pound fish was reported to have been caught by a poacher, with rod and line, on the river Nith in 1812, but the accepted British record for a rod-caught fish on fly is the one of sixty-five pounds by Miss G. W. Ballantyne on the Tay in 1922.

It is only occasionally that we hear of a fifty-pounder being caught now, but there are lots of fish over forty pounds landed, and fish over thirty pounds are just noteworthy.

I hope this outline of the life of the salmon shows what a wonderful fish it is, and what is more lovely to look at in the outdoor sporting field than a freshrun salmon covered with sealice?

It demands our respect.

2

Salmon in Rivers

A season's angling calls for quite a range of tackle, from heavy in Spring to light in Summer. Many rivers are fished with fly only and, at the moment, it is of these I think mainly. I prefer to fish fly for many reasons which will emerge as we go along, and I believe it would be very much better for the fly fisherman and, indeed, for fishing if there were fewer people spinning indiscriminately. There are many waters I know where little else is done but spinning, especially in the Spring. This is not a proven necessity to catch fish, but there is no doubt that to fish a fly in Spring is hard work requiring a high degree of skill. It is certainly not a case of casting a fly out as far as possible and hoping for the best any more than is the case with a spinner. An outstanding illustration of this showed itself a few years ago when I fished on the Driva, in Norway. On three pools, I was one of eleven rods and the only one fishing fly. I shall relate this experience more fully later, but suffice to say here that my fly rod produced four salmon and the total from the others was one — on worm. And none on spoon, spinner, prawn and whatever else might have been hurled into these pools!

Many anglers spin because they cannot cast a fly, and but for the spinning waters would be deprived of sport. I do not seek this. It is easy to spin in a manner which will catch fish, but not easy to cast a fly with a fly rod. This is a fact. Whatever one's beliefs about the effects on fishings and on other anglers, circumstances are not the same for everyone and we must all have our sport. It is a relaxing sport, when we forget our daily troubles. The fish can excite us and, indeed, exhaust us but the outcome is good — we have lived in a dream world a while and are refreshed. As anglers, don't let us irritate each other by the waterside. The rules are clear for the fly

9

man and for the bait man. There is plenty for all just now but, as
the number of anglers increases, the pressure on the available water
increases — more of it may yet have to come under fly-only
restrictions.

I have in mind a river where long casts may have to be made and
wading may perhaps be necessary to reach some of the lies, but not
so huge that boats are needed for fishing. The pools may be long,
without noticeable character, and where local advice is invaluable.
A ghillie will usually point out the lies and save you a great deal of
back-breaking work in high water but it is part of the day's
enjoyment and a test of knowledge to use all one's experience of
other rivers and pools to try and read the water correctly. Quite
often you have to do this anyway: a fair number of ghillies I know
recommend that you just fish it all the way down right from the
neck there to the tail of the pool, where the rushing water starts
again, or the trees stop you going any further! With a sigh and a
bracing of the shoulders you start right at the neck!

The season opens on some rivers as early as 11th January, so you
may be fishing in very cold, high water — even with ice along the
river's edges. Sna' bree, as it is called, is not good — this is when
snow and pieces of ice are carried down and the water has that
slightly cloudy clear look and ice forms in your rod rings and holds
the line. I do not fish then — the delights of holding a rod do not
come to me now until the weather is much more amenable but, if
this is your 'day', persevere. I have had fish in such conditions and
still wonder at it. The ice along the edges of a settled clean river
does not do any harm, but extra care is needed in playing a fish —
the ice is sharp and can cut your cast. At this time of year, I like a
quiet day with the light on the water dark and soft and friendly to
my eyes — with large snowflakes gently falling. If fish are in the
pool it seems to me they are always willing to take and it is up to us
to do our part correctly — to present the fly at the right speed and
depth, and do all the many other things we know to be right, until
the fish is safely on the bank.

On two occasions, not so long ago, I recall snow giving me some
unexpected trouble. The first was with a fish I left in the snow a
short distance from where I had killed it. The snow continued to
fall as I fished over the pool again. When I came to pick up my fish
I could not find it. The traces of blood were there and traces of my
foot marks showed where I had left it, but no sign of the fish. My

foot slipped into a ditch and I borrowed on twenty yards down towards the river — too near for comforting thoughts. And, then, there it was, stuck in some grass which had halted its headlong slide back into the river — dead though it was.

The other was when I was going to fish the river. I met a fine old man who knew it well, after a lifetime on it, but he was in failing health. There was snow on the ground — a crisp sunny day with cloudless sky. It was hopeless — no fish would come in this, he told me. I nodded. I went on and, by one of those flukes we all enjoy from time to time, I got a fish and put it in the boot of my car. Just then my friend drove back and pulled up — he knew it wouldn't be of any use. I could only agree — I had no wish to prove him wrong — and I thought he would drive on. But no, he got out to have a look at the river from the back of my car. There was blood on the snow! A quick shuffle, and my feet had it hidden! He was none the wiser, but my intention to avoid hurting his feelings very nearly misfired.

In Spring, the aim is to cast the fly well over the pool, get it to sink and swing slowly round close in front of the fish's nose. Variations of speed and depth are easily made and, as the water becomes warmer, these can be quite great but the basic principle is the same. You must always be in contact with the fly and have it 'fish' exactly as you wish; you and not the current must control it. I think blind optimism is bad. If conditions are bad, do not flog away endlessly and dull your judgment. The conditions can change suddenly and there must be enthusiasm to take advantage of it. It is a poor day, and a rare one, which does not give one chance of a fish, however slender. Some fish seem less highly educated than others!

A fourteen or even sixteen-foot rod with a heavy line and leader (cast) with an 8/0 fly or a three and a half inch weighted tube fly or an articulated fly to be cast twenty-five yards or more is hard work and, at day's end, can leave you in need of a dram and a rest. But it has never hurt a back so much as an hour in the garden with a spade, and never will! It is different somehow, and hard to explain.

Plastic covered lines are excellent — some float and some sink. The latter do not seem to snag on rocks as readily as one might expect. Some are very fast-sinking, but I do not like these as casting can be a little difficult. My good fortune is such that I have always had Kingfisher lines. They are unbeatable but, alas, now unobtainable. No doubt some firm will come along with a good replacement before too long. I hope so.

In the low temperatures, fish are usually taken from mid pool to the tail and not likely in the fast water. There might be one in the slack water at the side of the stream so, as the ghillie said, just you start at the neck.

Cast a short line down and across the fast stream at an angle of about fort-five degrees and let the fly swing into the slack at the side, keeping the rod low above the water, just less than at right angles to the flow of the stream, and draw the fly up slowly and evenly; you may have to stand a little way from the water's edge to do this if the slack is narrow. Do not point the rod straight at the fly unless you have slack line available to the fish before you strike. This is not easy when fishing a very short line, particularly if a single hook is being used, and even to a degree when a treble hook is on. The first few casts may be a little difficult because of the light weight of line outside the point of the rod and a false cast or two onto the water (not free in the air) may be necessary. Lengthen the line after you have fished out each cast until you have a comfortable casting and fishing length before moving down. Do not immediately pull out a good casting length when you start at the neck of the pool unless you stand far enough upstream to allow the fly to cover all the water.

Do not get rooted to any spot. You can make your cast and move down to the next stance — a couple of steps — provided this is aiding in letting the fly slip back the way you wish. I think it preferable to fish out the cast on the stance from which you make it and then move down, hand-lining as necessary. Have one cast per stance unless extra are needed to get the fly where and how you wish it, or to go over a fish again. As the stream slackens and the pool widens a longer line is needed. In order to fish the whole breadth, the rod must be held high at first to keep the line clear of the stream — difficult with a heavy line — and then lowered to the side to fish across the pool and one's own side of the flow. If the rod is not held high the stream will catch the line and whip the fly across too quickly. When the line is likely to be caught in the current and you cannot keep it clear by holding the rod high alone, give the rod a side flip to throw the line over and clear of the current. The fly will not be dragged away and it can be let slip back a little and go deeper. It can be made to hang over the lie and swing

Showing how to bring in a fish to net during an evening's instruction.

Start of a day from Culag Hotel, Lochinver.

Tackling up during morning's instruction by the river—ensuring rods properly assembled and knots well-tied.

Selection of fly is important—a bright fly or a dark one, and which size? The day's sport can depend on the right choice.

The author's daughters, Lorna and Barbara, started young and in difficult territory.

Note the 'black cap' of the kelt. A kelt must be returned to the water undamaged and it is important to hold it on an even keel head upstream until it is ready to swim off.

The author with two fine old ghillies, Peter Stewart and Hugh 'Begg' Sutherland, and a young one, Hugh's son Marcus, at Altnaharra.

Pointing out a good lie where two streams meet in the neck of the pool; a difficult return from the stance when a fish has been hooked.

A long cast, without apparent effort from the author, showing how the line is brought forward in a narrow loop.

across river as you wish. Take care in switching the line over in this way — not too much power in the movement lest you pull the fly as well: it must not be moved in this 'mending' of the line.

The side flip or 'mend' can be made immediately after the cast and before the line sinks — if it is sunk the movement tends to draw the fly up and across in a way opposite to what is desired. A good mend is a continuation of the completed cast. Sometimes an angler is seen giving little flips in additional mends as the line comes round, moving it only a few inches — with doubtful influence on the fly. It is possible to let the fly slip back, beyond the current, by letting out a yard or so of line at the end of the mend — and often the only way to get over a lie properly.

A fish is not always greatly attracted by a sinking fly nor by one that is becoming shallower, so try to have it pass at an even depth in front of the fish. When the cast is completed, let the fly swing across the flow, keeping the rod point low and still, so it seems that the fly must stick on the bottom. This is often the difference between success and failure on a good many days in a season. Do not handline, except in preparation for the next cast, nor have the rod dipping up and down even if it may 'put life in the fly, sur' or, as I view it, give it convulsions! Still, it is good to do so sometimes in slack water and as a variation — be it only for your own satisfaction. I believe an early fish prefers a steadily moving fly. If I do handline while the fly is coming round, I let the rod point slip back enough to almost counter the draw and, between draws of the line in, move the rod point back to maintain an even speed, which is slightly faster than if it is allowed to swing round entirely as the water speed dictates.

Fish down to the very tail of the pool, where there may be a boulder making a lie; you will see the bulge in the water caused by the change in flow from it, just as the water speeds up on its rush down to the next pool. A 'touch' may be felt, or a momentary sensation of drag on the fly and no more — do not strike or speed the fly on its way, just fish out the cast quietly and make another to bring the fly round exactly as before — if nothing happens, rest it for a minute or two and repeat the offering. It may be a kelt or a clean fish. It is seldom a clean fish does not have a second go, though there are remarkable exceptions which I shall refer to later. It seems to me noticeable that early fish travel in pairs, so look for the other! Many find the best taking times for these early fish are from noon to 2 p.m. — but do not be careless at other times — and again, as the daylight goes: do not stop too early in the day.

Many pools are long and slow-running and the recommended way of fishing them is by 'backing'. As with the most slow moving water, a ripple is best, if not always essential. I like an upstream wind while many others prefer one downstream, a subject discussed more fully when considering the use of finer tackle. Usually, the pool is fished down from the neck as far as the stream is strong enough to bring the fly round. The angler then goes to the tail of the pool. A long cast is made almost straight across but slightly down. The rod is held firm for a moment or two to let the fly slip into the start of the arc it will make across the river. Four or five short slow steps are taken upstream, with the rod point low, to keep the fly swinging round. A turn is then made to face downstream, and the line handlined until the fly is brought right in, and up what may be deep water by the bank. Fish may take at any time in the long swim of the fly. The next cast may call for a false one to get the line out again and this inconvenience is an almost unavoidable result of fishing out the previous cast to the limit. It is not always necessary.

I have caught many fish this way but I prefer to work down and make my handling produce the same movement of the fly — I do not like repeatedly splashing a line (and this can happen with the best!) over a fish before asking it to take my supposedly unattached morsel. Nor do I like walking along the bank and perhaps disturbing a fish before trying to catch it. Nevertheless, it is a productive method, and many ghillies will be displeased if you do not use it where and when they indicate. Backing is done throughout the season, but my objections to it grow as the more delicate techniques come into use.

Provided the temperature is not too low, a high water usually means fish will go on to the main headwaters of a river, into deep pools or a loch; they will do so also in cold water, always provided that there are no waterfalls or undue rapids or shallows to navigate. Fish are not at all keen to run in low very cold water, or any water with ice and snow in it. Yet not always so! On several occasions in each of two years in early Spring, fish ran a river when I am sure they did so against all natural tendencies. We caught fish at the head of the system, all fresh run, while only one or two were caught in the river below, with none showing. We had two very dry late Springs and Summers these years and I wonder if the runs came on quickly, while the going was there, though not to their liking, knowing or suspecting a drought. These running fish did not take any offerings from many experienced anglers on the river. The slower running fish especially will take a fly at his nose, preferably a large one, even in Summer, while he is resting a moment or two.

The slow-moving large fly close to the fish's nose, needed to stimulate any response, suggests the fish is a bit dull in very cold water. Early fish tend to take the fly very slowly, in a lazy turn while opening and closing the mouth. One angler believed in putting his labrador through the pool to arouse the fish and another put a large spinner through it to make them take a fly later. Trolling with an outboard engine churning the water above and ahead of the bait may do good in the cold deeper water in a loch. In Canada, a flasher, almost as large as a biscuit tin lid, is trolled ahead of the bait. Some of this may have the desired effect but I have not found a large spinner through a pool improve the fly fishing in it afterwards. I much prefer to fish undisturbed water, even if my dog might, at times, benefit from a swim through it! This dullness seems to change to signs of alertness about forty-one degrees Fahrenheit and this increases as the water temperature rises to about fifty-four degrees, though it returns as the temperature goes higher. The variations in temperature in some rivers can be quite great in a day and good fishing times vary with them.

I recall a pool I used to fish with prawn in mid-March — a deep black pool, with high sides of sheer rock, I fished it patiently a few times before I found I had to pass the prawn down round a point of rock for just twenty minutes before a fish would take, and then I would get one or two. It was the same in high water in this same pool, with worm — patience was rewarded. One day a friend came to speak to me there and I laid down the rod with the prawn only six inches in the water. We talked a very long time (I don't know how long, really, but any fishing time wasted talking is long). I had forgotten about the rod when there was an almighty splash fifteen feet below us. The reel gave a turn and the rod bounced. A fish had taken the dangling prawn — it wasn't hooked, as there was no resistance to drive the hooks home but, nevertheless, the happening suggested annoyance and attack, rather than reflex action to take and eat. Perhaps it presented itself as a possible competitor at spawning time?

As the days go by, the water becomes warmer, and lighter tackle and smaller flies are used. The change from a heavy line (which must be used to get the fly down to the Spring fish) to a floating line is too gradual to be decided upon by using a fixed water temperature, say forty-eight degrees, as the moment for doing so. Each year I hear words of astonishment that someone had caught a fish on a floating line and the water was only forty-five degrees or so. I have had salmon, in February, rise to the surface and show in the take, like summer fish, on several occasions to the very large fly when, by most of our rules, it should not happen so. This is not the contrariness of the fish so much as a further example of what we have yet to explain. It was the fly on the surface that made the fish show, though it was very cold for it to do so. Was it the light, the temperatures of air and water, speed and depth of fly, the size and colour of the fly or other unknown factors, which triggered off this action to take the fly? As the water warms, the flies used are smaller and fished nearer the surface and, mostly, moved faster.

One Thursday evening in an April long ago, when the river was high, but in good order, my father caught three lovely fish. It was late and there was too much of a rush to get home for me to have a turn with the rod. I pleaded to be allowed to fish next morning but the thought of accompanying me so early did not appeal to anyone. The river was too high and dangerous and I was too young and too wee to go alone, and that was that! But an old 'uncle' gave me the wink that he would fix me up. I knew he would not come with me. I was glad of this because, if I caught a fish, my family's willingness to suggest he had hooked it for me would be great, albeit in fun. I wanted none of that! I had no need of a morning call. By six o'clock I had collected rod and flies and was off hot foot to the pool, three-quarters of a mile away. It really was exciting, and I am sure it could not have been so much so unless, subconsciously, I knew I would get a fish — or thought I would. I knew the despair of losing a fish and catching nothing all too well. I had the rod up and ready in a few shaking moments. There wasn't much time. There was a lot to do. A two-mile journey for milk, a breakfast to eat, and preparations for going to school.

I started at the neck. It was a short pool with shingle on my side and a steep, tree-lined bank on the other. The river was at a height when it was more of a stream than a pool but it looked beautiful to my eyes and I continued to shake. I blinked as I felt sure I saw the swirl of a fish at my fly, a Jock Scott. The swirl did not last enough for me to be truly convinced it was a fish. I had only my longing memory of it. It had vanished downstream, like that snowflake. I didn't cast again. I knew I must rest it. Would anyone believe I really had risen one? I fretted and fidgeted for an hour, or maybe it was just for a minute, and started again. And there it was! I had him! I don't seem to remember much else, except bringing it in on its side, getting a quiet grip of its tail with my right hand, dropping the rod from a fair height and getting my other hand round its tail. I gripped well and carried it over the stones and far from the water, though with several turns to clear the line from stones. The fish did not kick until I put it down. I killed it. I sorted out the rod — it survived its drop — and struggled to pick up the fish but could not manage both. It was huge. I left the rod — I could come back for it. But not the fish. Not my first salmon on fly! I carried it home across my arms and had everyone in the hotel on their feet before 7.30 a.m. But not my uncle! I told him quitely, as I thought he might like to lie low awhile. The fish was twelve and three-quarter pounds. I then did my chores. It seems a very long time since I caught that fish on that Friday fifty-odd years ago. I shook with excitement that day and with fish many times afterwards. Alas, the thrill has largely gone now, but I get great joy in being with someone who does get this excitement — as happens very frequently for me.

Smaller flies are used as the water temperature rises — at least such is the general rule. But some rivers may need a fly size 6/0 to produce results while, on the same day, not many miles away, a size 1 may be the right size. Indeed, some rivers need size 4/0 in July and one pool, in particular, perhaps an 8/0. A rule for choice of fly and size is difficult but, elsewhere, I refer to a fly size chart which is an excellent guide to your starting-fly size.

It is good to get rid of the heavy line as soon as possible and to use it only occasionally, as in very high water or on stormy days or in late Autumn. If a rod of fourteen feet is not a stiff one it may be used with a comparatively light line to great advantage when the river is in good order, or slightly lower. Casting this light line is not too much of a problem so long as it is remembered that the weight of line outside the point of the rod is of critical importance. With a light line, a greater length is required than with a heavy line, to give the correct weight necessary to make effective casting with any particular rod. The longer light line out means a slightly firmer casting power and a slower movement as it straightens out in the back cast. I shoot line during my back cast to give me this correct weight. It is not so difficult as it may sound if you watch the line straighten out behind — a skill you must learn if you are to have your back cast go in between branches of a tree, without becoming caught up.

A light twelve foot or twelve and a half foot rod is good for the time when the fish are coming to the smaller flies on, or near, the surface and a fine cast is used. Farlow Sharpe of Aberdeen make a delightful twelve footer for me — impregnated cane, light and supple, and a joy to use with the light line — designed for seatrout, grilse and salmon. A number two Kingfisher line is ideal for it though I often use a number one. Casting is a little different from that with a heavy line but it is easy to learn and, for me, the angler who cannot cast with it naturally and become adjusted to it with a few casts is neither a good nor a stylish caster. My years of close association with a vast number of anglers make me believe that seventy per cent of them are very poor casters, very inefficient in handling the tools of their sport. The knowledgeable fisherman who is a good caster is a better angler than the equally knowledgeable one who is a poor caster. Casting well is a part of the skill of the good and successful angler. Please forget the contention that 'though I only cast a short line I catch as many fish as the next man, who may cast a long line'. It is what you do with the fly when you cast it out that is so important. And the wider the area you can cover with a properly-fished fly (or bait), the better will be your bag of fish and the greater your pleasure. I have many reasons for liking the long rod: ease of casting and mending the line, fishing the fly as I wish (particularly when 'fishing the dropper'), playing the fish, keeping clear of snags in the water and bushes behind, and for numerous other reasons we'll notice as we go along. The light outfit allows great sensitivity and control.

A few hours I had on a river one July which brought me my most fish on fly in one day will help to illustrate this. It was half past ten when I set off with the ghillie. My host had fished on ahead of me. I did three pools and landed six fish before going on to join him for lunch at noon as arranged. He had one. At two o'clock (imagine it!) we set out. I had to go and watch him fish a run with his great fourteen foot greenheart rod, heavy line and thick cast. The small fly looked as if it was on the end of thin wire. He rose a fish but the long delayed action striking was more than the fish could stand and it ejected the fly in good time! There was no feeling or control between angler and fly. He sent me off with the suggestion that I had better not catch more than ten, lest his rental be raised. He was a guest in our hotel and I could not comment as I felt wont. I stopped at ten past three with my total at ten. He joined me at four o'clock — his ghillie carrying one fish. My ghillie did not know how to hide his shameful delight. Oh, my host did not mean I should stop fishing — not really. He would go and get the car and I would have a cast or two in the pool he had just fished. He would be back in five minutes or so. I did. Two more fish came my way. I cannot imagine what my bag would have been if I had fished more than these few pools, and all day. And all because I fished fine tackle with a little knowhow. Both my host and the laird tried casts I gave them, similar to what I had used. Both hooked fish and broke. Both condemned my method. They used their heavy rods and heavy lines. They could not cast without them. Too often all too true, I fear. The delicacy needed to use these with a fine cast was more than they could produce. I did not lose anything by it all, but I was disappointed for their sakes.

It was about 1927 that I first began to realise how very profitable it was to 'use a dropper' for seatrout and salmon on a loch or river. This realisation developed until I found the top dropper, properly fished, would yield salmon which would not be caught by any other method of fly fishing I knew. 'Dibbling', as it is called, has the same effect, though very limited in its range and not the same as 'using a dropper'. I know there are many fellow anglers who will raise their eyebrows at the very suggestion of fishing with three flies on the one cast for salmon.

That renowned angler, Major the Hon. F. Ashley-Cooper, said that, given suitable conditions, there is no doubt that the skilled use of a dropper fly adds greatly to the interest and excitement of fishing and that, further, it does increase the bag. Two flies on the cast, fished properly, must increase the amount of water covered at each cast. Another fine angler, Mr G. M. Hancock, gave his opinion that a dropper attachment is a source of weakness in the cast and, when playing a fish, the unattached fly may become caught in snags. In practice such disasters have been found to be infrequent and can usually be attributed to carelessness; there is also the danger of hooking two fish in one cast but the advantages far outweigh the disadvantages.

I would ask critics of the use of three flies on a cast for salmon to pause a moment and recollect when they tried it out for themselves. Did they know how to use such a cast and did they give it a fair trial? Surely it is not a failure because it did not produce results when tried, tried, perhaps, with a faulty technique. Surely the method is not to be condemned because of the risk of one or other of the free flies becoming caught on a rock or snag, while playing a fish. That risk is very small indeed and only once can I remember having lost a salmon in that way, and that was due entirely to my own carelessness. I have landed many salmon, not just a few dozen, which I would not have risen unless I had been fishing with three flies, and that on a number of rivers. I have also landed many seatrout over eight pounds and quite a few* seatrout of ten pounds and over without difficulty with the three flies.

However, I have often foul-hooked other salmon in a river while playing one. It was an all too frequent happening at a lie in one particular pool in the river Garry. First time over in the morning, the tail and middle flies, which were sunk, would be refused and, when the dropper came over, up he would come, take the fly and turn down with it, firmly hooked and nicely done. A moment later, the serenity was gone and another fish was off down the pool as fast as reel would unwind, with the tail or middle hook in his body somewhere, and the dropper gone. It was usually landed eventually and I have finished by getting the third one hooked! On several occasions I have risen two at the same time and while this and the foul hooking are not held to the credit of the method, it is a minor disadvantage, far outweighed by the pleasing results of the extra fish caught through it. Two flies only might lead to fewer fish being foul-hooked but they do not allow the dropper to be fished so well or so easily. These events can hardly come into the category of deliberate foul-hooking, which is so easy if it is one's intent.

I remember, in 1944, playing a good fish which showed nothing untoward in its fight but, as I brought it in to tail, gliding on its side on the surface, it seemed held for a few moments, as if the tail fly

* 1928—12½ lbs. (oldest known)		1930—14 lbs.
1931—10¾ lbs.	1939—10¾ lbs.	1939—10½ lbs.
1943—10 lbs.	1943—11 lbs.	1943—13½ lbs.
1953—11 lbs.	1958—12½ lbs.	1959—10½ lbs.
1966—10 lbs.		

had got caught up. This held its head and it rolled over, broke the cast and was gone. But a smaller fish, of sixteen pounds, on the tail fly, came straight in for me to tail, hooked in the mouth and played out. Luck was just against me as they were both played out and the real danger time was past. I feel sure I would have had both of them if I had known sooner and planned the final stage accordingly. This was a time when the gaff would have been used to advantage! The first fish took the dropper beautifully. I don't know when the other took, but it had ample opportunity to do so.

With a cast of three flies, the tail fly fishes as would a fly fished singly. The centre fly comes nearer the surface and care is needed to avoid having it make an undesirable underwater wake: it is a perfect guide as to whether or not the cast is too thick: fish will always turn away from the fly if it is too heavy. Naturally, I suppose, as the fly is beside a double thickness of cast and this cannot be avoided. They will rise 'short' to the tail fly too if the cast is too heavy. Usually the size of fly is changed, whereas it is often the thick cast which is to blame.

It is the top dropper which brings the great results. It has been used for a long time, certainly all this century. Perhaps it was developed from 'dibbling' of years gone by when 'winches' (reels) were rather primitive and horse-hair lines of limited length. 'Dibbling' must not be mistaken or confused with the fishing of the dropper fly on a two or three-fly cast. The dibbling was done with one fly only and it is used still with effect. Some call it 'dapping', which is unfortunate because dapping is a quite different way of fishing.

My host on the day I caught twelve gets most of his fish by dibbling. He has the long rod and, with a short line, he dibbles the fly directly in the streams and white water, holding the fly dancing on the surface. He strikes when the fish has taken the fly, has turned, and is well on the way down again. In playing it in a way not recommended, he grudges every inch of line it takes! The heavy line and cast he uses is no disadvantage, and he likes to 'lean' on the fish — his own expression.

But to return to the dropper. Draw it across at right angles to the stream and it will rise fish which have refused a fly presented in the usual manner. If it misses the fly, it will almost certainly rise again and again until it is caught or has touched the fly or cast or been disturbed for some other reason: I rose a grilse one day eleven times before I caught it and there were only a few seconds' rest between each rise. Times without number I have fished down a stream with a cast of three flies just as I would with a single fly, and risen nothing until I was opposite the lie with shortened line bringing the dropper across it. This seldom fails to bring the chance of a fish in ' fair' conditions.

Often, others have fished immediately ahead of me but this has made little difference, provided they did not scare the fish by wading carelessly, splashing a heavy line over them, putting a shadow over them or disturbing them in some other way. One, scared fish can spoil the whole pool in a few moments, with fish jumping in all directions. Don't let such jumping fish tempt you to keep thrashing at them. Go and look for an unwary one: it is there your real chance of success lies. Fresh run fish are not so easily disturbed as fish which have been up for a time, but it is profitable to treat them all alike.

When I say to bring the dropper across the stream, I do not mean a mostly useless 'bobbing' across. Bring the fly across so that it makes a steady wave — a V — against the current, and vary the speed at which it is brought across with successive casts. By this 'wave' I mean the steady wave a quarter-submerged fly makes and not the undesirable drag an almost completely sunk fly makes, as when the fly is not tied on properly and hangs obliquely, instead of straight. A dropper treated with dry fly solution is as unsatisfactory as allowing a drag on your fly, when fishing a dry fly. An undesirable bubbly effect is, produced. I prefer a large dropper fly — size six or even larger.

Fish may well be caught in the ways I do not recommend, but I have tested them well before condemning them.

A light line is essential to get the 'dropper up' and to fish with this wave: a heavy line drops in to the rod and draws in the fly too quickly. I like a steady upstream breeze best: it helps to get the dropper up much farther across than is otherwise possible, and more of the stream and pool is fished. It helps to keep the flies from slipping back with the current and forms a belly in the line in the air which helps in hooking fish. A gusty wind makes it all more difficult. Fishing with just two flies does not give sufficient drag to get the dropper up so easily, either on the loch or the river, and an extra-long leader (cast), to give this pull, is not a happy solution.

I always use as light a line as possible, not only for the extra sensitivity of contact with the fly but also when it is necessary to have the fly hang for a moment on a lie far across the stream, perhaps at the tail of a small pool where the lie is very narrow, or just a short black glide in otherwise white rushing water. There are many small lies to be found in similarly awkward places in most tumbling rivers and it is possible to cover them and fish them with the long rod, holding the line high and perhaps bellied out and clear of the currents. It may be necessary to fish such a lie from a stance higher up river than usual and cast a long line more downstream to the lie: a good mend and the fly will be kept where you want it long enough for the fish to take. It is the kind of lie we come across so often and which waterlore teaches us to spot. The fly must hang long enough for him to take or it will be whipped away by the stream, and all you see is the fish's tail turn, far behind the fly. There is a limit to the speed with which fish can take, and they are reluctant to go right into the fast water.

When Autumn comes, larger flies may be needed and fish readily take a fly made to hang over them, and one swinging slowly and evenly across. The main stock of fish at this time are coloured, getting ready to spawn, and not the treasured prizes we all seek. But there is always the chance of a silver fish in any river in Autumn — some have good runs well into November. In fact, it is likely that most of the large rivers have clean fish entering in every month of the year.

The cock fish tends to take a larger fly than the hen in the Autumn and, in rivers where hens must be returned at this time, I use the largest fly effective, for this reason. The tails of pools are good taking places, but the flow of the current as it glides smoothly down may be faster than you imagine, so do not 'hurry' the fly round. By this I mean bringing your rod point round with the fly as it comes across; not only does this speed the fly on its way, but it lets the fly slip back downstream. The use of the dropper can bring results in the streams, in stretches and slacks, not usually fished, between pools and into which fish move as the season of spawning approaches. Whether you are to strike the fish properly in the case of a cock fish or to pull the fly away before it has turned in the case of a hen, is a decision based on experience.

We return to more general aspects of river fishing. The day may be bright, the water lower than you would like and you are unable to fish before sunrise. Then, look for shaded pools and runs. There may be a hill or some trees or even a bridge which shades the lie for a time in the morning. Fish it with care, for chances may be few on such a day. There may be a lie which will be shaded later in the day: reserve it. Such tactics can of course be adopted only in areas of peace and quiet. Develop an ability to predict what is likely to happen, based on reliable principles developed from years of experience.

In such bright days, a short time before sunrise and again after sunset, fishing can be good: with good water, blinks of sunshine can help sport, but not a dazzling sun glaring back at you off the water and not when it is shining directly downstream.

There was a marvellous pool I used to fish which illustrated two things well. First, on the brightest of days and in low water — conditions too adverse to attract poachers with rod and line, stick and garden line or net — the little stream was shaded from the sun by a rock and some bushes until about eight o'clock. It gave me one chance only in the day but yielded many fish when every other stretch looked and was hopeless. Second, when in good order, it invariably gave me the chance of three fish and, often I caught the three — one from each lie. I started, with a short line, and crouched low at the lie near the tail of the twenty yards' long stream which opened out into a long deep pool. A wide shingle was on my side and rocks and alders on the other; and away down river, slopes of birch on both sides ran down to the shingle and rocks. When I rose and hooked the fish, it seemed its natural escape was down into the main pool, where it was played out and tailed. This left the neck of the stream undisturbed though, on occasions when a fish did return to its lie — as so many fish do when they are being played — a steadily applied strain prevented unrest in the area and a little more pressure from slightly upstream persuaded it to move down into the main pool again. The same was done at the second lie, half way up the stream, and again at the third lie in the very neck. A normal careful start at the head of the stream almost certainly meant one fish only from the pool. A careless start meant none.

I remember, when I was still a wee loon, going to fish a river for seatrout one day in August. It was fairly low and I took an eight-foot rod which I had been given as a present some two years earlier. I had always fancied using it, but my father, who knew so well what might be hooked, insisted it was too light and short for the river and certainly for me who found casting an easy way to break a rod. I would not be told and had to find out for myself how unsatisfactory it is to use such a rod. It is not that there is any difficulty of casting a sufficiently long line in open spaces, but it is impossible to fish the fly properly in many rivers. The line cannot be mended nor kept clear of the stream to hang the fly over a distant lie, nor can a fish be played as it should be: a stone protruding above the water or a small bush has to be passed in keeping line to fish clear and keeping up the dropper. When a large fly is used, seldom is any fish which may be risen hooked: the single hook cannot be firmly embedded unless the rod is pointing directly to the fish, line given and the strike made more or less by hand. The sight of an angler playing a fish, with one arm holding the rod up to the skies and the other hand stretched up and groping for the reel far above his head, while the eyes are focused on the fish or line somewhere down below, is ludicrous — continued to the next stage where arm is high and hand out low with net not quite reaching the fish! There are plenty of photographs of famous fishermen to show it all so. No doubt a great golfer could play a round with a putter but he would not: each club has its use and so has each rod. I fret at so much talk of using a small seven-foot wand of a rod for salmon — pure American humbug! Many years ago I had the greatest of satisfaction in having a great man in British casting, who was equally obstinate in this respect, being finally enlightened on this matter by the little river Kirkaig! Remember, seldom do I let a picture of a river such as the Hampshire Avon come to mind as I write: I think mainly of the healthily flowing Scottish rivers.

That particular day with the short rod the pool looked very nice — the stream came into my side and just over it was a deep stretch that went all the way to the tail, perhaps forty yards, before the river widened to a steady rush of two or three feet in depth between a two hundred yard maze of large rounded stones washed clean with the flood waters of the past. On the far side of the very neck of the pool, I brought the dropper across the stream — expecting the rise, and it came — a finnock. I struck, missed, and with the flies in the air well behind me, my 'finnock' rose on: head, back and tail, and, oh, so slowly — a thumper of a salmon. The white of its mouth had deceived me. I tried it again but with no response to two offerings. I rested it and changed to my favourite of all salmon flies — a Jock Scott on the tail to replace my number one seatrout fly, a Peter Ross. I had only an OX (seven pounds breaking strain) and I knew I was being a bit foolhardy but, I was a mile from home and even on my bike, I wasn't inclined to go too far from my fish for too long! I started again. Second cast my flies came over and stuck: there was no rise, no break or movement on the surface of the water — nothing! My flies had just stopped. I struck, but nothing happened. My rod just bounced back — lucky for me because, when I struck in those days, one or two things were liable to happen — usually a broken cast but sometimes a broken rod! The fly might have been stuck in a rock for all the life there appeared in it. My heart was sinking and I was beginning to fear the worst, when slowly the line began to move up and I knew I was into the fish. It played in the pool a long time, then turned and went down into the wide stretch of rough water, whitened by its rush over the many big boulders. The fish played hard at times but it did not make any wild rushes. The rod was much too light and short for this kind of work — and so was the cast, but I took all the care I knew and they met the demands made on them. A roadman, long since gone, bless him — Bama by nickname — watched all that went on and came down to help me. I had the fish played out and lying on an even keel behind a rock, in the slack water, and decided I would get him to hold the rod steady, exactly as I gave it to him — and not a finger near the line. I waded in without waders (they were expensive and it had never been suggested I should have a pair — my boots, stockings and legs used to dry off satisfactorily!). It was fast water, and the stones did not give much of a foothold, but I got there, tailed the fish with both hands and got back to the side and well away from the water's edge safely. It was my most difficult tailing to date — and a fine fish of nineteen and a half pounds. At home that night I was nearly made to believe that Bama had got it out for me with a graip!

The light on the water is just as important for river fishing as for loch, and perhaps we do not pay enough attention to it. A softly falling snow gives a marvellous light. Some describe a good fishing day as a good growing day and so it appears. But only with high cloud and absence of low mist. Yet I have had many good days when the mist has been low on the mountains, with the wind and rain and conditions of absolute misery! Those heavy, sultry, thundery, headachy days of Sirius — the dog days — enervating days — are seldom good for man or fish. When you look through untinted polaroid glasses, the light on the surface of the water is soft and easy on the eyes and wherever you look there is no strain to contract the pupils and wrinkle the face. Every movement on the surface of the water is seen from afar but the fly is hidden and the bottom of the pool not seen. At times it is easy to see the fly in the water a long way off but I never found fish to take well when it was like this; it is strange how the fly does show up some days and yet not on others which seem to be exactly similar.

Polaroids are comfortable to wear but their penetrating quality makes it so easy to see fish in pools that one is tempted to go and have a look before fishing in the pool. A stale fish may thus be disturbed, to rush through the pool or stream and unsettle a clean fish, making it rise short rather than well; a taking fish lying near the surface may sink deeper and become a non-taker. With polaroids the tendency is also to go very much nearer the water than realised — if you take them off you find yourself in a most conspicuous position. Polaroids encourage one to strike too soon, but, perhaps worse for me, they give the impression of the light being good all the time and lead to long periods of considerable concentration. I do not like this deceit and must see the light as it really is, as it changes greatly, quickly and frequently, in a day.

At rare times the light can be excellent, when the fish will take and you must accept the chances given. At others it is bad and time to change a fly if you must, but do remember a clean fish might surprise you, so do not just cast and droopingly hope for something! Even on the very worst of days I believe I get at least one chance which might give a fish if I had just that little bit of extra knowhow. There are pools on many rivers which fish well no matter what the light is, generally with rocks and mounds and trees to save it from the worst. A hard glaring light with a dull sparkle or an ink blue reflection of the sky, or a glazed leaden colour, do not raise one's hopes of sport. Whether the light which appears so bad to us gives extra good visibility to the fish so that they can see all the falsity in our offering or not, I do not know: it is strange how, in a very bad light, a fish is sometimes disturbed when it would seem it should not see anything. There is an answer somewhere.

In our concentration on variables such as air and water temperatures and the state of the barometer, we may neglect the very important factor of light. On certain days in July I have known a grilse to take a size 2/0 Silver Doctor when it would not rise to a conventional size and pattern for such conditions. There may be there are many other flies they would take. As with many another angler, I am sure, I have seen a sharp heavy shower change the whole feel of the day and fish begin to rise almost immediately in pools previously fished and 'with not a fish in them'!

At seven o'clock one May morning in 1945, I set out with my wife on a six and a half mile cycle ride to fish — as indeed I did every morning except Sundays. But this was a marvellous morning with very high cloud, thick and soft, with the whole countryside clear and easy to see, without the imminence of rain — we felt good, with the pedalling ahead a joy to come. I said as we went along I would get seven fish and that was more than ever before. All I ever imagined would make an ideal fishing day had come together. The water was perfect and the light was gentle. From every pool a fish. Seven, none under sixteen pounds, and all on fly. Quite a load on a bicycle! I rose an eighth but did not strike. I had enough and, to this day, my wife, angler that she is, does not understand my contentment with the seven. It had been the perfect day. Strangely enough, I had seven on several occasions that season but could not get an eighth though I hooked and lost five times — poor reward for my earlier consideration!

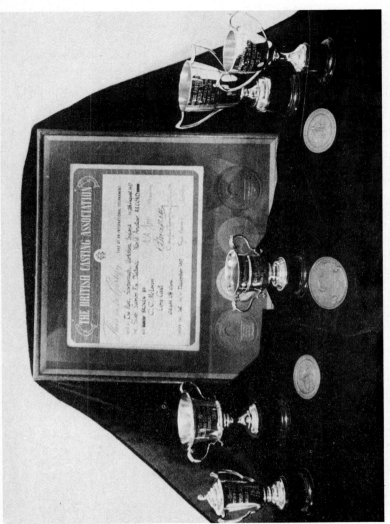

Some casting successes in Scottish and British Casting Associations' Competitions.

A 'Steeple' or almost vertical back cast from a precarious stance:
it is necessary to shoot line and the large fly required adds to the
difficulties—the Kirkaig Falls Pool.

An awkward position high above the fish; they are difficult to hook from such a height and there is no lower stance.

The author fishing a good pool on the Kirkaig. The lies are on the far side of the stream at this height of water and casting is difficult.

Too high or too low water can make this stretch impassable by fish, but even at a suitable water level it is a rough run for them.

Jetties forming new lies where previously there was only shallow water, but often a new pool is made at the expense of the next pool downstream.

The result of a well-spent hour and a half on a favourite loch, fishing lies which had not been fished for many years.

Loch Naver—a delightful loch and one of Scotland's finest for salmon.

3

Salmon in Lochs

As a general rule, salmon lie in much shallower water in a loch than do seatrout — with a good wave breaking onto a shore I have seen them caught regularly in only two or three feet of water. When it is calm, they are in their main lies in a depth of five or six feet and where those which have not moved in will rise well in a good breeze. But an off-shore breeze is not good and this may be because the boat, being in such shallow water, and the oars perhaps hitting the bottom, disturbs them. Or they may not like following the fly into the shallow water. Although I have had a good many from the bank of a loch and still get some from time to time, it is difficult in a gradually deepening shore and casting into a strong wind. Many fish follow and turn away. Try to find spots where the water deepens quickly and the fish is able to rise and take before being drawn into the shallow and shying off. The same thing happens in a river when a fish turns away as the fly is drawn on towards a rock.

Salmon lies are usually to be found off rocky points, at largely submerged or partly submerged rocks, at river and large burn mouths, or on 'banks' by these, where shallow suddenly deepens, or in deepish 'holes' in shallow bays near a river. They lie, too, in places we cannot see in detail and without any characteristic to suggest a lie, but where they find a place of comfort and rest. As time goes by we get to know these places well — a fish may be caught in a spot, clean or kelt — or may be seen to jump regularly at some point, or may be risen by a rock or clump of weeds or river mouth. These are lies forever as far as we need care, unless the river mouth changes or lies get filled in with sand or shingle carried down by spates. It is a safe assumption that, if the river mouth changes — where it 'plugs' into the 'lake', as an American friend

described it — the lies will move with it. Do not be deceived by
running fish, which may jump anywhere — out in the middle or
close in and not in lies — it could lead to a lot of extra fruitless
fishing. An angler may fish a loch many times with a ghillie and
yet, if he had to go out without one, he would not cover the lies or,
indeed, anywhere near them. He is not a rarity and this is all too
often the case on a river, too. So take note of all the marks and
features on the banks, and take bearings if necessary so that you
will manage alone if need be. Some can remember well all the good
points, weed banks, shallows, rocks and so on of all the many lochs
they may have fished, perhaps only once. This comes naturally to
some, but, with a little application, all can remember some of
them, and that is a start for the day. When the fish are up, a salmon
lie usually has a salmon in it, so approach it carefully.

Before the war, I fished the head of a beautiful loch frequently
for salmon, char and seatrout. I knew the times of the tides and
runs of fish and when the char would be on the surface. In 1960 or
so, when living a little more than a hundred miles away, I had a
yearning to return for an evening about the end of May. I could
combine a turn at both char and salmon though it was almost
impossible to choose a good evening weatherwise at such a
distance.

I asked for a boat but none were on the water as it was too early
in the year to fish. However, the longing I had to return to haunts
of so long ago must have been felt by the owner, as he very kindly
agreed to put one out for me. It was a great joy to be going back
there. A friend I was to meet did not turn up on time and, at six
o'clock or so, I decided to go out for a while — I might do better
alone, anyway — to lies I knew and others I would guess because
the river had changed. Two people in a boat make more
disturbance than one, and I have firm views on how easily fish can
be disturbed at times. My care may have been rewarded and they
were there waiting for me, seemingly as dim as only salmon can be
at times. I caught four in an hour and a half, on fly, before going
back to wait for my friend. Next day, I took him out and put him
over fish he rose but could not hook — until he did get one
eventually, hooked by the tail! All in all, a fine experience spoilt a
little by an envious keeper saying I was poaching his water (though
it was too early for it, too!) and my friend's remark that fewer
salmon might have been killed if we had not been fishing for them,

while waiting for a char rise that never came, and had concentrated on salmon only! I thought he had failed enough as it was! We used to get fish in March (and twice in February) but no-one knew of the runs. We caught char in plenty: in 1939, one day on fly, my father and I had one hundred and eight char weighing a total of sixty-four and a half pounds and, yet, one caught in 1956 or so had to be sent away for identification! Wherever you are some old ghillie might be able to recall what is valuable information of days long ago and, even if it is only hearsay, it is worthy of investigation.

When the water temperature is still low, but with the fish in from the deep, use a large salmon fly from a boat, using a long line. Draw the fly from the shallow into the deep — this is done most effectively when the boat is being pulled very slowly along parallel to the stretch being fished. The fly swings round in an arc, which seems so much more tempting than coming straight, and a risen fish is easier to hook. A really good wave is needed. It is easier and better to have the angler fishing over the stern of the boat — sitting on the first plank thwart from the stern or, better still, on a secure plank across the gunwales. He is then able to fish downwind all the time and the ghillie, despite the huge wind-catching areas of the high back in front of him, can keep the bow slightly to the side of the wind and work along exactly as he wishes. If a fish is hooked, the boat is pulled away and the fish landed without disturbing the lies. If one is risen, it can be tried again without having been disturbed by the boat going over it. Do not 'hog' a good spot — move on and let other boats have their turn and hope the occupants know what they are doing and not let the boat disperse the fish from their shallow taking lies. It takes a long time of peace and quiet for them to return and be settled — it might be night before they do.

If it is a bright day, keep off the lies and leave the fish quiet until a little while after the sun sets: there is a time when salmon will rise and take, unless it is dead calm. A good swell and fading breeze is best of all at that time. Dry fly can be effective in the calm and dapping in a breeze — but more of that some other time.

A good seatrout fisherman will catch salmon as well as anyone but the reverse is not the case. Seatrout demand the best of all the skills. Please do not misunderstand me: salmon fishing demands the very greatest of skills and art but it does not encompass the

wide variations called for by seatrout. I know the salmon angler
often catches a damned nuisance of a seatrout when he is expecting
a fish, but that is a frequent chance he runs, not because of a skill he
has. Quite a few I know disclaim seatrout fishing because they have
never had the thrill of really taking up their challenge, perhaps
through a lack of knowledge or skill or opportunity. A famous man
said to me once — and he is a fine salmon angler — 'Fish for seatrout one day and you have got to rest them for two days before
they will rise again'. It can be nearly so but not if you have the techniques of a seatrout fisherman, who would never have that opinion
of salmon! I hear the same niggle about many who can cast a long
line: this I do know is because of the critics' own complete lack of
ability to do so. My friend who lost a forty-plus pounder was a
prime example.

As the temperature of the water rises, salmon will come to the
seatrout size of fly and the best way is to fish for them exactly as for
seatrout. In some places where there are weeds, it may be wise to
use one fly only so long as it is effective, but, otherwise, use a cast
of three flies or, if the flies are larger, two flies but 'fish' the
dropper. It is often at the end of a drift for seatrout that a salmon is
risen: they are usually in shallower water and I who unashamedly
think seatrout finer to catch than salmon, used to end the drift
before coming into the salmon water.

I may have a guilt complex about this — catching a salmon can
rather spoil one's seatrout fishing. A long time ago (1928 or so) —
and so much seems to be long ago now — I helped out the tenant of
a very fine loch by keeping the boat for his party. They did the
rowing as I was still too wee to row it much, but I did know the
drifts and kept it on them. As a reward for doing several days of
this — in addition to a little financial benefit — the tenant, Mr
Morrel, said I was to have a day's fishing and if I caught a salmon
he would give me a present of a rod. My father, brother and I went
out and took turns of fishing and keeping the boat; immediately
after our brief break for a 'piece' about two o'clock I hooked a fish.
I knew it was a good one but none of us saw it. I had an eleven-foot
reinforced greenheart rod — reinforced with a crisscross tinsel-like
whipping its full length — a supple rod but fortunately so as I had
only a 1X (six pounds breaking strain) cast on. We saw the fish —
another huge thing — on the tail fly, a Peter Ross. No-one else
could fish while I play it for an hour and twenty minutes before

my father tailed it. We went ashore as soon as we could after I hooked it, otherwise we might have been there all night! Seventeen and a half pounds it was. We did not rush to claim the rod — we did not mention it. But in the Spring of the next year my rod arrived — a beautiful split cane twelve-foot Farlow rod. At the outlet to the river from that loch there is a huge square of rock where the water is deep just as it draws away — a marvellous lie for salmon in April and May. There are similar lies in many lochs.

Farlow Sharpe make my twelve-foot rod of their impregnated cane and the design is based on talks I had with Pierre Creusevaut and Charles Ritz while my wife Barbara and I were their guests in Paris and at Amboise, where I had the pleasure of seeing a small but important recommendation of mine being incorporated in the Pezon et Michel salmon rods. I use it with a light line and at least one hundred yards of backing so to be free of running out with one of those fish which takes off smartly and goes a long way before the boat is on course after it. I remember having a heavy seatrout (ten and three-quarter pounds) go far out into the loch, leaving me on the shore with all my line out — not a turn left on the drum. (I had already been up a tree in order to follow it!) I waded in as far as I could and, with the waves splashing a little higher than I could fail to notice, reached out the rod to the limit. There was nothing more to be given from my end and, out in the distance, I saw a great tail in the air, as the head was held and the fish turned over to be brought straight in and tailed. I was never caught short of line again.

It is easy to cast the comparatively short distance required from a boat and, after making it, pause for a count of, say, four seconds before raising the rod point slowly to bring the dropper steadily along the surface, making a nice wave for the last third of the draw. The final yard or so of line may be handlined in to avoid having the point too near the vertical, where the danger is that the line falls close to the rod and, when a fish is risen and struck, the angle of pull on the rod is so acute that the tip is almost certainly broken or severely strained.

Do remember that a fish can take the fly properly and yet not be felt. The line goes out or, rather, straightens slightly, but nothing is felt, possibly because, after the rise and take, the fish continues slowly in the direction of the boat. A call from the ghillie is unlikely to allow for the strike to be made in time and, indeed, the call often brings the reply that the fish had not touched! Maybe so, but the ghillie has a view from a different angle and he is used to such things; better to strike first and discuss the outcome later.

Too often, anglers have returned at night with a tale of fish rising 'short' or rising just as the flies were being lifted off the water for the next cast and the reason has always been the same — the flies have been drawn through the water too quickly and for too short a time, an unavoidable result of trying to fish a dropper with a short rod and heavily tapered line. A salmon will sometimes rise right under the gunwale of the boat but turn away at the sight of it, as on to a rock or into shallow water.

The apparent solution is to cast a long line and draw it in slowly but this is not truly so. There is a lot of line in the water and, unless drawn in quite quickly, the flies will sink deeper than wanted, even with a floating line. The speed at which the boat drifts onto the flies has to be more than neutralised; when two are fishing from a boat, it is normally drifting broadside on a guided course downwind but, for choice, better to take turns on the oars and one fish over the stern. As it is handlined in, there may be all sorts of coils and kinks of line on your knees, or in the bottom of the boat, perhaps round a floor board or foot, or just round a coat button or the rod end or reel handle! It can happen quite unnoticed and give an anxious moment or two when a fish is hooked. Try a long rod — it will solve the problem.

To see a salmon rise and take, through a wave, is a memorable sight — far greater than the joy of any rise on a river.

4

Striking Rises

To strike or not to strike? YOU MUST STRIKE. A firm raising of the rod point, and a properly timed tightening of the line, must be made so that after the fish has turned away with the fly, the hook is secured in the fish's mouth over the barb. It is not a violent or near frantic, albeit involuntary, strike which flashes the rod back with more force than either it or the cast will tolerate. This tightening, which I prefer to call a 'strike', is a short and convenient term for the act of making secure contact when the hook is pulled in the mouth of the fish. It varies with the type of rise, the kind of water being fished and the tackle used.

There is no controversy about striking when fishing from a boat. Always strike, but know that every strike has its own correct timing. There is the immediate strike for a 'line go', to the long wait which must be lived through for a slow head and tail rise. Or no strike at all, as when a fish misses and the flies are drawn steadily on for the fish to rise a second or third time, or takes or touches the fly or cast all in the one draw. A strike which snatches the fly suddenly often deters a fish from rising again. You may catch a glimpse of something — and a fish is on and being played without any conscious strike. At times, the line may seem to 'go'— the belly in it seems to straighten but there is no boil or movement on the surface of the water to indicate a fish. Strike at once, as when a 'boil' is seen. There is no time to wonder if it is a fish. Strike first and consider later! A drifting boat moves towards the fish risen and the fish may come towards it, so there is no chance of any pull on the line though the fish is travelling with the fly in its mouth. Only a firm strike through a larger than usual arc can hook it.

Striking is an art needed less now in the days of treble and quadruple hooks than in those of the single or double-hooked fly. The last has never been a favourite of mine and, though I do not condemn it, nothing has been demonstrated to me to show any advantage it may have. The single hook has to be struck home against the turn of the fish: no give of line or ease of rod to allow the fish to turn — otherwise no fish. It is wise to think in this way with the multiple hooks, too, but I have seen many fish hooked and, mostly, landed, when the rod has been pointing straight downstream to the fish and not an inch of line given at the rise or draw of the take. It seems many anglers 'get off with murder' in their hooking techniques. All is usually well, so long as the fish is not immediately held, with little use of the rod to soften the heavy strain.

When a long heavy line is out, with a large fly well sunk, the first indication of a 'touch' may be that unmistakable message, though a little remote, passed along the line to the hands holding the rod. Or the line, where it curves into the water, may tend to straighten. Have no hesitation — strike! But never, after any strike, hold hard against the fish — keep a firm strain only and do not begrudge line. You cannot expect to hold a newly-hooked fish in a stream if it wants to go down with it, unless your tackle is unduly heavy and the hook with a solid hold, which may be hard to find in the soft mouth of a fresh run grilse when hook holds are often slender. When the rod point is directly downstream, line must go free to let the fish turn down or away with the fly before it becomes the right moment to strike.

An aim in bringing the fly across the current is to have it do so without slipping back downstream. If the rod point is brought round — thus hurrying the fly across — it means the fly will slip back by that length. It may be the rod must come round to bring the fly directly below you, in which case you are probably wading too far out. Handlining as the rod comes round prevents the fly from slipping back and gives ready line to release at a take. I prefer to hold the rod low and at right angles to the flow of the stream whenever I can: the belly in the line, the give in the rod and a momentary easing of the rod point towards it, is enough to let the fish turn and have the hook ready for securing in its mouth.

Do not be tempted to strike a second or even a third time to be sure the hook is home — a doubtful but often used practice and, I think, a dangerously mistaken one.

I like a free running reel, though of course not one that runs off and overwinds. The line is passed between the index finger and cork handle of the rod. This is necessary when handlining, and it is easy to release enough line for the fish to turn. Coiling the line round fingers and thumb in the delicate, elegant way of the trout fisher is not recommended. The finger presses the line firmly to the rod to hold it tight for the strike and it allows for an excellent control over tension when playing a fish. A time when I leave the line completely clear is in anticipation of a rise when casting out from a boat as it is being rowed along fairly fast — a fruitful time over the years.

Polaroids help you see the fish rise but lead to extra moments of that supreme control you must exercise for the slowly rising fish.

I believe a salmon means to take the fly when he sets out for it. It may be he has doubts as he leaves his lie, but these can be dispelled or increased as he rises. The idea I have of the fly or lure sparking off a reflex action arises from a suggestion of it I heard long before the war — it is not new. I want to keep hasty theorising, and my imagination, under control but prefer the latitude to form opinions based on sound principles which appear over the years, and to accept and work on these until better come along.

Some salmon take a fly without any inhibitions and are very easily caught at times by a good angler. At other times they are extremely difficult. If a fish sets out to rise, however slight that movement in its lie might be, we should catch it. The reason for failure is what we have yet to learn: some anglers are farther along this road of learning than others. The fact that the fish inhibits its urge to rise, or rises and does not touch the fly or even open its mouth, means something we are offering is wrong — the fly or the technique — and a defensive reflex action takes over. Too large a fly, too thick a cast, an earlier fright or warning of danger, too fast a fly or one too slow and deep, or for no apparent reason: the fish remains safely in command.

The Falls Pool on the river Kirkaig called for very large flies to bring fish to the surface. A small percentage would take the fly but the vast majority would glide under or past, like small sharks but with mouths closed. I wonder if this dark pool, in a great hole, with cliffs of rock rising sheer from the water to form a funnel of spray, produced a light which needed a large fly to move the fish from the lie, but which became too large as the fish approached it. A

possibility? In the rest of the river I had fish on large and small flies
but it is, essentially, a river for the larger fly.

A fish which has touched — or has 'interviewed', as someone put
it — the fly or cast may need a good rest before it will come again.
A Spring fish may give a good pull and not be hooked and, next
cast over it, take well and be caught. Perhaps the low temperatures
of Spring deaden the senses a little — or is it his travelling com-
panion which takes second time round?

When a floating line is used, the fish, which is usually seen, must
be allowed to turn down or away with the single hook fly before
making a strike graded to the strength of the cast. There is little
belly in the line to allow the fish to turn and line must be given to
let it do so. The difficulty is less when the rod point is held low to
the side, or high when reaching across a stream, and can ease
towards the fish to give it line. It is also rewarding to strike thus
when a treble or quadruple hook is in use — a retentive hold is not
always adequate.

Rises in calm water or with too light a breeze can be frustrating
— there is a limit to the lightness of the tackle which can be used. It
is better to leave the lies completely undisturbed until a breeze does
come up, or evening makes the light wind sufficient.

It is difficult to hook a fish risen when one is standing high above
it — on a high bank or from a bridge. This may be because of the
angle of the fly in the water. I have overcome it in many places
from a bank, by going far upstream and keeping the rod point low
to let the fly lie as horizontally as possible.

Another rise which can be a heartbreak is when the wave of a
fish following the fly shows and both seem to be travelling at the
same speed. This often happens, especially when drawing into
shallower water. Do not stop the fly — speed it up and be ready for
the fish turning with it. Do not be hasty with the strike — wait for
it!

A very strong wind may create a situation where the fish is seen
to rise, and even take the fly, but the power of the wind so bends
the rod that the force of the strike does not effectively reach the fly
and drive the hook home. A strong gusty wind is even more
difficult and uncertain. The rod should be held low to the water to
keep the line out of the wind, pointed towards the fly, and line
given at the rise. The strike comes in the first part of the curve in
the rod bend, and so is less affected by the wind. The fly can be

blown away from the fish at the critical moment in a strong or gusty wind when fishing from a boat, the bank of a loch or on a river. These are the days for a stiff rod, with point held low.

The presentation of the fly over a lie in a way which makes the fish come up in a hearty head and tail rise, and the perfect strike to click the hook home as he goes down, is now my greatest joy in fishing. But it is the end of my own pleasure in dealing with it. Sharing the excitement of another playing it and landing it has long replaced the fun I used to have in doing so myself.

5

Playing a Fish

After the firm tightening of the strike there is a momentary lull and the fish may stay just a moment, quietly, before moving away, or it may be off in a rush, pulling the rod down and the line off a reel screaming in protest, even before a strike could be contemplated. There are many variations between these two extremes. The type of rise usually gives a warning of what to expect, but not always; and not all takes are seen. So we must be ready — no loose line round coat buttons or reel casing or the like to check, with a jerk, a sudden rush and leave us in despair. We make many casts per take.

The response to being hooked probably arises from the speed at which the fish rises to the fly or takes the lure and where it is hooked. A slow rise and slow firming of the hook in the fish's mouth does not immediately put a great and sudden pull on the fish and make him lunge off against it — so the start of the playing may be sluggish. On the other hand, the hook may well be in a place which causes him pain — in parts of the mouth or, if foul hooked as so easily can happen, in the eye or sensory nerves of the lateral line, when he will surely streak away at great speed; it is usually when he makes a fast rise or turn to take, that this happens; but not always — a slow rise can lead to seeming pain, too.

These uncertainties have to be borne in mind all the time and linked with the kind of tackle being used. In Spring and high water, it may be heavy and the risks of breaking with a fish are small, but in low water, with fine tackle, the risks are considerable.

When a rod of thirteen feet or more is being used, the balancing tackle is usually heavy but it is not always so — sometimes light lines are used. These matters and the use of floating lines are discussed elsewhere.

The well-sunk line means a rise is seldom seen. The line goes, the belly in it straightens, the rod is firmly raised, with only a click from the reel, and the fish is on. The rod is held high, at eighty degrees or so, with a good bend on it. The line is allowed to run free, without great strain but sufficient to keep the hook held firmly in place in the mouth — a complete slackening could let it drop out. The reel can be adjusted to give whatever tension is desired. I feel able to control this and vary it more efficiently by having the tension of the reel set lightly and applying pressure on the line between my index finger and the cork handle of the rod.

Line which is loose between finger and reel or in coils from handlining must be wound on to the reel and, while there is still time, it is wise to get on to dry land or easy walking territory if wading or on some precarious stance when the fish is hooked. It is only then you are in a good position to combat the ways of a fish feeling pain or the pull of the hook against which it is fighting for its life.

The fish tends to move away steadily as extra pressure is put on it. Often a change in direction of pull from the angler can change the fish's route but, when it is already hellbent on going somewhere, it is unwise to seriously dispute this intention! It is well to keep the line as short as possible, and easier to exercise control if the angler keeps opposite the fish whenever possible — a few steps down or up can change the angle of pull to upstream or downstream. It is good to be below a fish if there is any danger of it going down out of the pool. Alternatively, the line may be lengthened and eased a little to have the belly caught in the current and give a pull from downstream.

The strain must be firm and steady, with the rod point high and well bent so that the springiness of the rod is in the circuit and no harsh, hard jerk can cause a break. Whatever the tackle, it is well to allow as little line as possible to be deep in the water, and to remember that the more there is in it the less pressure should be applied with the rod. When the fish is far away and a lot of line sunk, the line must be allowed to run and give the strain, rather than let the strain come from the pull on the sunken bellied line as it is straightened — and which is so hard to regulate. The fish needs only to go off with a rush after a fright from touching a rock for the strain to become excessive if the line is not left free to run. It is almost as disastrous as a wild leap or somersault when the rod point is not immediately lowered, to prevent the overgreat strain of lifting and straightening the sunken bellied line — which happens when the rod is held high at such a time. Too often a fish is seen to leap out, but the strain is so much from the drag of the line, with the rod held high, that the head is held and the tail flies over — and all is lost.

When a fish is on the surface splashing and kicking — in deep water as well as shallow — and when it is 'jigging', extra care is needed. The full springiness of the rod tip must be used and this comes from holding the rod lightly but firmly at an angle of eighty degrees or so. But no nearer the vertical, when the angle of pull is so acute that the springiness is lost and, indeed, the tip snapped. I learned this in one or two hard lessons with greenheart rods more than fifty years ago.

There may be more fish lost by being too light on them than being firmly persuasive with them. Playing is a persuasion making full use of the currents and eddies and, indeed, the seeming contrariness of the fish. The fish almost certainly feels the restraint more than the pain and reacts to it. When the pressure is eased, the fish will stop almost at once, unless it is running away fast, when the drag of the line in the water keeps pull on it. A fish will lie in a stream for a long time when steady pressure is held. The hook may be in such a position that the pull is against the angle of the jaw, when the current catches the forward part of the head. This gives an otter board effect and the fish tends to go across the stream, away from the angler; little effort is needed from the fish to keep itself in that position and there is no variation on the amount or direction of pull to disturb it. The otter board effect can happen in still water from the angler's pull alone. This may be the case at 'sulking' spells and I think it happens in many cases where fish are 'played' for hours on end. I remember being asked, a long time ago, to go and help the laird's wife, who had been playing a fish for many hours — it had not moved from one spot since it went into a tiny cauldron in a pool below what was called the Ladder Pool. I felt the rod and the soft tugs which were thought to come from the fish but were only the waves of water catching the line and giving this effect. The line, or hook or cast, was caught in a rock and the fish had gone. This water effect on the line is deceptive, but the deadness of the pull through it is quite unmistakable to anyone who has felt it frequently. A delicate position for me but, eventually, the 'fish' was lost and commiserations spread all round! So beware.

I have been involved in many instances of fish and angler being locked in battle at either end of the same line for many hours, mostly with the fish eventually gaining its freedom. It helps to keep us informed as to the tremendous size of some of the fish in the river!

I recall an occasion when I went out to the river Kirkaig with the afternoon tea picnic which had been forgotten by a party of fishers. It was half past three and when I reached the river I saw that 'himself' was playing a fish — or else the fish him — at the Old Bridge Pool. Missus was at the Elder Pool casting away, and I drew her attention to the battle that seemed to be going on two hundred yards upstream. She was not impressed — the fish had been hooked at eleven o'clock in the forenoon. It is not a habit of mine, but I am sure I rubbed my chin. I went along, and signs of renewed hope, or something, appeared on his face as he saw me. Would I hold the rod for a minute while he went into the woods? No, no! I had come across disasters before! I got him to move downstream and change the angle of the pull — it was a huge fish, thirty or thirty-five pounds maybe. A spectator thought it forty pounds at least. Perhaps we would know soon. Slowly the fish moved to the neck of the pool, was startled, turned downstream and passed us at a fair lick — to freedom! 'Ah, well' is all one can say. I thought it as well to agree about the possible size, and forty pounds it was. Not an ounce more — until I heard about it later that evening in the cocktail bar! I don't really think that anglers are liars, but perhaps they do tend to exaggerate a bit at times. The nylon was frayed where it had broken at the hook, and who would wonder after constant wear for over four hours, even if the strain was only light. I am sure a firm strain would have played out this fish in reasonable time. I learned a lesson here.

Not long afterwards, perhaps a couple of days, I went to fish another river for a short time one evening, after dinner. On arrival, I saw my Kirkaig friend, leaning forward with his rod bent and a fish on. I didn't want to spend my precious hour as a spectator again, so I nipped down to the pool below, the Star Pool, and on the right bank. I caught a salmon and a seatrout, took them up to the car and then went on to join my friend. I applied some pressure on him and I eventually netted his three pound seatrout. He was using nylon of ten pounds breaking strain — my seatrout cast was of seven pounds break strain! I wonder, did it save him from losing another forty pounder — or was it fifty?! In this case he was standing upstream of the fish and just holding it in the stream, he himself getting more and more tired but saving the fish from any effort to stay in the stream. The longer a fish is on, the greater the chance of losing it. If you dictate the way it is to be played, it is seldom you will lose it. There may not be any rules to cover all fish but they do respond to certain tactics.

Some take off downstream, set on returning to the sea right then. They must be followed and the long line recovered to the maximum extent and as quickly as possible. If you cannot follow, you must act quickly and before the fish has left the pool, anticipating that it intends to do so. Lower the rod, let the line slack, pull off yards from the reel and let it go so that it is caught in the stream and taken beyond the fish, when it will give pull from downstream. The fish's instinct is to fight against the strain and it will turn upstream again. So we hope, and such is usual, but the odd one does carry on and all we can do is hold and dream of the possible.

Fortunately, many of the fish which go to the tail of the pool turn on the very edge of the rough water below and come back slowly. I do not think they really want to go down but too much extra strain at that time or the turn of the reel or a jerk can make them go. So just raise the arm and rod, and quietly free as much line as possible from the water. Now walk gently and evenly upstream and he will be led along, perhaps on the far side of the current. He can be taken far up to where it is safe to resume normal tactics, away from the dangers of encouraging a downriver trip. This is one of so many instances when the user of a short rod has extra problems.

A fish can feel the vibrations from the reel being wound in at a great distance but particularly so with a short line, as when bringing it in to shallow water or to net. At times, the response to this winding of the reel is such as to make it unwise to do so. When in this situation, do not wind in but, instead, take a few carefully chosen steps back, and the fish will be drawn towards you. Whenever intending to 'walk' a fish in this way, or 'pumping' it, always let it steady itself and not be fighting you before applying the little extra pressure to 'walk' it along or in. You may be on a stance or site when you cannot take a step back and it is now that a 'pumping' action of the rod solves the problem. Lower the rod slowly, almost pointing towards the fish, and at the same time, wind in so that no vibration is transmitted along the line. Hold the line firmly between index finger and rod handle, so that none will slip out, and raise the rod point smoothly, with fair strain, to the vertical. The fish will come along. Repeat this manoeuvre until the fish is in the position you wish for the next stage of the encounter.

Keep in mind the fish's contrary response to the pull on the hook and try to take advantage of the streams and eddies and rocks and shallows. When it is in the stream and tiring a little, it may be in need of a moment's 'breather' and turn in towards you to ease the strain and for respite. Recover the line quickly so there is no lessening of the strain and lead it on into shallow water by making it come round in a wider arc and more quickly than it had intended. It is thus involved in extra exertion by its natural response to shallow water or some fright.

Do not let it rest or be still for more than a few seconds as it will adjust to the angle of pull and settle where the minimum of effort is called upon. If it does do this it puts you in the position where extra pressure has no effect and you become more and more apprehensive about the strain your tackle will stand. This can lead to hours of frustration, final woe, and, maybe, with it, physical discomfort. There are many true tales of anglers being in contact with fish for hours on end and having to be plied with food and drink to keep their body and spirit in one and having their route lighted by a small torch.

Deep pools have their own problems, but do remember 'pumping' and 'walking' can move many a dour fish. Change the angle of pull to upstream or down or sideways, but never with jerks. Tapping the rod butt with a stone sometimes helps. And encourage any however slight movement of a sulking fish by pulling in aid of the move. A stone can be thrown in to try and disturb it but, though it may not seem so, the risk of striking the cast is quite great — so great, indeed, that I throw it so far away I doubt if it does any good! A fine cast struck by a stone breaks like thread, a risk to take with your own fish but not somebody else's.

In the days when Bogie Roll was in so many waistcoat pockets, I remember my father, in time of need, used to fix a small, weighted coil of it round the line and direct it down to the fish's nose. The fish's response was usually the one wanted, but whether it would have liked Condor and stayed put, or have equally disliked a coil of twig, I do not know. No doubt the tobacco became the chewing supply thereafter.

Occasionally a fish will run out of the pool, upstream. Beware of this. He frequently turns as he tires at a rock or big stone, on the upstream side of which, in fast water, there can be an eddy. I have seen salmon lying apparently head downstream in such a place but they are in fact head on into the up flow of the current at the bottom. The fish usually chooses to turn into this eddy and comes down on the other side of the stone or rock, leaving your line looped around it. It may come down fast with the line from the reel ripping upstream. As the line lengthens the strain increases; the fish may come to the surface and show near you, far from where you expected it to be. The only hope is to go up and release the line, hoping the fish will stay on while you do so. A long rod is an advantage.

Of course, this doesn't happen always, and the fish may turn and come straight down, without any drag on it, swimming at full speed and with the aid of the stream. It is hard to take up all the slack and keep contact. Handlining in great pulls is the only way, and speed in winding up the slack afterwards is vital. It is the only occasion when I feel there might be some advantage or use in a geared reel to the average angler. The fish may not turn, and it may stay head on to the stream and slip back slowly in a most co-operative way.

It is strange how, on occasion, an almost played out fish will ease its way across a stream and show itself in the shallow on the far side of the river, sometimes to get snagged in the stones. When it tires further there it gives in to the pull and can be guided steadily by the angler right in to the side for netting or tailing.

At the end of the struggle it may be brought in several times before it can be netted or tailed — it may be frightened off by the sight of the net or by touching the bottom. When it turns away, guide it on and bring it in again. Do not try to hold it and stop the turn. Remember the cast may be frayed or weakened and the hook hold loosened or torn and too weak to stand a strong restraint even if the fish is played out and only the force of the current drawing it away. Turn with it downstream, keeping the rod to the side and not too rigidly held.

Is it any great wonder that so many anglers, when playing a fish, become quite different persons from those we knew — shaking, sweating, incoherent and oblivious to all else? But it does them all so much good in the end.

Nowadays, and for many years, playing a fish has few joys for me, but I still get a great thrill from hooking a fish and seeing the excitement of another playing it. I like to pass the rod to someone else to play the fish, and it is surprising how often fish are lost at this time of hand over.

6

Gaffing, Netting and Tailing Fish

We are almost at the end of playing the fish and we concentrate on the last stages of bringing it in for gaffing, netting or tailing — whichever method we choose.

Over the years I have noted with interest the number of anglers, including men of long experience, who, when they go salmon fishing, simply must carry a gaff. There are times when a gaff can be useful and occasionally a necessity, but the indiscriminate gaffing of every fish, irrespective of the conditions, cannot be accepted. I seldom use a gaff, and in all the waters I know, there are few places where I could not land a fish without one. In my young days I was not allowed a gaff and just had to learn the art of tailing fish by hand — all sizes of seatrout, as well as grilse and salmon.

You may be lucky enough to have someone carry your gaff or tailer or net, but a long-handle gaff or net is a positive danger to your very life when it is slung over your shoulder and dangling about your legs as you jump from rock to rock or walk through rough country. It can be caught in shrubs. As often as not, it is left at the head of the pool and far from where it is needed, or perhaps forgotten and left two or three pools back. A tailer can be difficult to get over your shoulder and off your back, but it is usually kept there and not left behind. A short gaff is almost as unsatisfactory, and is usually in some inaccessible place when you want it — in your bag or under your coat, or behind your back with a difficult catch to undo! This short type has a telescopic handle and has to be extended without damaging the point, which must be sharp; the sole of your wader is at risk when you use your foot to help extend the handle — no danger with care, but your boot can be pierced at this time of excitement. A gaff can, of course, be useful with a large fish or in awkward spots where a net would be difficult, as in trees or jagged rocks. My largest fish was not a monster — only thirty pounds — but I managed to tail it by hand without any undue difficulty.

I do not like to see gaff rips in various sizes almost anywhere on the body of a salmon. This ruins the appearance of the fish and means a loss of blood and pinkness from the flesh, as well as making a bloody mess. It is better to preserve the beauty and quality of fish by netting or tailing, and if the fish is to be sold, one gaffed is of least value. In some rivers the use of a gaff is prohibited at such times as when kelts may be caught or when fish are nearing the spawning stage and should, of course, be put back, though this is of doubtful value.

The fish is best gaffed while it is on an even keel and quitely swimming past under the control of the angler. A good quick gaffing is done while you blink almost — but there is no guesswork in it. The ways of gaffing a fish are varied but the traditional one is best — put the gaff over the back of the fish, behind the cast and just forward of the dorsal fin; reach a little down and beyond it and, with good power, sharply pull towards you and so stick the gaff, at right angles, into the fish's side. As it is being lifted out of the water, the hand and arm must be turned inwards, putting the point of the gaff uppermost; as the fish struggles, it puts itself further on the gaff. If you do not do this, and the point is left tilted towards you and downwards, the fish will certainly kick itself off the short leg of the hook of the gaff. The whole is held up and away from your body so that the fish will not strike against anything solid and bounce off. It may be gaffed in the head or near the tail or in the middle cut — or, in some cases, wherever one happens to get it! Try not to gaff it in the belly as this can make a big and unpleasant gash. Do not snatch at the fish as it splashes. All too often I have seen repeated attempts — rapid scraping-like movements — made to gaff a kicking and splashing fish before it has been secured or knocked off the hook or the cast broken. Quietly does it. The angler has to bring in the fish steadily and say when he wishes it to be gaffed. Yet some expect the ghillie to get out in the middle of the river after it! My advice is not to wade out to disaster. Picture what I have seen happen: the fish has raced between the gaffer's legs, been deeper in the water than thought when gaffed, and stronger, or the line caught by the gaff. If the fish is lost, it is your fault, whatever may be said!

I recommend a net with a large metal frame, almost a complete circle but with, at its distal end, a short straight section of nine inches or so. It should have a long and strong handle but still be light in weight. I do not like the folding type because the leather thong or the chain which holds the net out in position from the metal arms sags towards you as you push it through the water beneath the fish being brought in. The fish appears to be well over the net but, all too often, when the net is lifted it is found that the fish is balanced on the section of thong or chain.

A large net is best of all for landing a fish, particularly if you have someone to carry it for you. Otherwise it can be more of a nuisance than a gaff. In deep water or by a steep bank it is invaluable. The played-out fish, lying on its side, is led over the outstretched net so that, as it is lifted, the fish drops in. Or it may be led swimming into the net. In a stream or glide, swimming but losing ground, the fish can be let slip back tail first into the net. There must be no panic, waving of the net, or excited leaping around: all the movements are quietly and smoothly synchronised so that the fish is in the net before it knows what has happened. In shallow stony water or shingle the straight section of the net rim lets it be held low to get the fish in. It is heavy to lift a net with a fish in it at arm's length, so, with the fish enclosed in the net, draw it towards you, then lift with one hand at the handle end, and the other close to the ring. If the fish has grounded, it is easier and safer to hand tail it.

In a boat, it is usual to play the fish on the windward side of the boat. As the fish is brought over the net, the angler may relax the strain, to let the fish drop into the net. If it has been forgotten that the boat is drifting away from the fish, and it is only partly over the net ring, it may fall out as you lift, assuredly with hooks from the sprat or spinner tackle, or free flies, caught in the net! Yet I have known of fish which were lifted into the boat dangling in this way! Do not be tempted to have a swish with the net at a splashing fish. The hold of the hook in the fish may be weakening, and the strength of the nylon failing, but, as the seconds pass, don't despair. Just take care.

The metal tailer is an alternative. It has a wire loop which has to be set to 'trigger off' as soon as it passed round the fish and pulled. It tightens, and the body or tail is then held in this secure snare. The loop is passed over the fish from the tail, and it is not always easy to do so. The long handle and cable to the snare, and the length of the fish, means a very high lift to keep the fish's head clear of the ground. A long strong arm is needed to hold it so. It is not my choice, but it does not damage the fish.

I prefer to tail my fish by hand whenever I can and I usually must, as it is only on special occasions I have a net or gaff with me. I admit it does take a little longer to get a fish in, but what of that?

The fish is seldom ready to land first time brought in, so beware as it rushes off at the sight of you or as it touches a boulder or, in some way, is frightened: be alert to this and let it run. With the short line, the reel will disturb the fish, so, for the last few yards in, do not turn the reel but walk back or take a step or so, or use the pumping action. You may handline in evenly but there are risks involved in doing so: a sudden demand for line might find it caught on a button or round the reel casing or handle, and that means possible breakage of hook-hold or cast.

Always keep the rod to one side or the other as you bring the fish in — it avoids pulling the fish's head out of the water, when a shake of its head can be disastrous, without the impedance of the water to soften it. The fish should be led or glided into any convenient spot, head first and lying on its side, about a rod's length from you and with the rod at an angle of about forty-five degrees. Never draw the fish straight in towards your feet, unless trees or obstacles leave no choice: the outcome is a vertical rod and a danger of snapping the top piece. In shallow water the fish will lie quite still when it is brought in. If it is kicking, ease the pressure until it goes quiet again. If it is brought in to the left, have the rod in your left hand and so, with the left arm slightly extended to keep the strain steady, move up to the fish quietly but purposefully, bend down and catch it by the tail with the right hand.

Take care not to shorten the line more than a foot or so before you move to pick up the fish. I recall a friend demonstrating the result of doing so, quite unintentionally: he shortened the line too much, and as he moved towards the fish it was pulled on ahead of him. I do not know how far he might have gone had a bush not caught the rod tip and bent it to end the pull!

The accepted way to grip a fish, at the thin part above the tail, is with the thumb and index finger next to the tail — that is, with the hand supine. This means putting the other fingers under the fish but it allows a very secure grip. I never use this technique, I'm afraid, except in deep water, and I have always found gripping the fish, with my hand prone, perfectly safe. When I was young and my grip not so firm, I used a handkerchief which I had soaked and squeezed as dry as possible. This was spread on the palm of my hand before I took hold of the fish and it meant a good sound hold. Perhaps, now that I am getting older, I may have to call in the aid of a handkerchief again. But not yet!

Once the fish is gripped, lift it high and away from your body, turning your arm in as you do so and, when it kicks, tighten your grip, but allow your arm to swing with the kicks. If you try to keep your arm rigid the fish will surely kick free from your grasp. The grip is made by the thumb and index and middle fingers only. With a very heavy fish — one too heavy to lift and hold with one hand — grip it well at the 'wrist' above the tail with one hand, gently ease the strain, lay down the rod quietly and get both hands round the fish at the tail and lift it up and away, well back from the water. The fish will wait for you to do all this, if you do it calmly.

I remember when my late brother lost the first fish he had caught when he was alone. This was at the Manse pool, a difficult place on the river Gairbhe in the Ewe system. (There seems to be a Manse Pool or Minister's Stream on every river! The clergy must have been keen anglers or valuable friends of the lairds in those days!) He tailed the fish but, as he was carrying it high in front, up a steep bank, it slipped from his grip; he fell forward on it but, with a couple of kicks, it was over his shoulder, down his back and into the river. He could only watch.

Excited grabs or jumps, or other antics as you approach the fish, are sure ways to trouble and, unless you are very, very experienced at doing so, do not take hold of the line to pull the fish towards you if you are tailing it for a fellow angler. It is a temptation to step into the water and be between the fish and its likely way of escape. Some time ago now, I was told by a very well-known angler about a fish shooting off between his legs to freedom. Fortunately he had only one fly on his cast or he might well have been left with one or two in his leg!

When the water is deep it is sometimes not possible to glide the fish past so that you can slip your hand underneath for tailing. On these occasions the fish may be tail down and head up and it is relatively easy to slip your fingers under the gill cover and lift it out.

When more than one fly is used and the cast with free flies lies along the body of the fish, be sure to grasp under the cast so that, if the fish does slip, there is no danger of being hooked in the hand.

'Beaching' is a method of landing a fish advised by some well-known writers, but I cannot see any virtue in it or reason for it. You can judge for yourself. I give my observations in parentheses. Many rivers have suitable places for beaching — a gently sloping shingle, sand or even rock slab (ideal for tailing a fish). As soon as the fish can be made to come into the shallows the angler, with rod held high and a steady pressure on, should walk slowly backwards until the head of the fish is out of the water on the shore (a degree further in than is needed for tailing). Thereafter he must wait, keeping on the steady pressure until the fish kicks (and puts great strain on the hook hold and cast, whereas it would have been tailed by this time). He will find that each kick works the fish higher and higher up the bank (or has broken the cast or hook hold). Then, when the whole salmon is clear of the water, the angler can take off the pressure, walk forward and pick up his fish (and tail it!). Another form of 'beaching' is to get behind the fish and push it up to safety (or tail it) and, being behind it, a fall on it can be made in an emergency — all very delicately done (and then tail it!). Well?

Do not be tempted to do this with grilse, which have the reputation of being impossible to tail. They are a little more difficult and a little more care is required, but this idea has arisen mainly from some who have not used the right technique and perhaps been a little impatient. Small fish of three or four pounds are not really 'tailed', but gripped at mid body.

Whoever is gaffing or netting or tailing a fish must never have his face in a line where, if the hook was to break its hold, the fly would come whipping out and into his face. This can happen very easily and it is too grave a risk to ignore; a lost fish is nothing compared to a lost eye.

A net, then, is best, but all will be well so long as you have your two hands and a handkerchief and keep calm. It is good to take home, admire, and display the unspoiled beauty of a salmon.

7

Wading

The other side is always the other side, whichever side you are on, so there is no real need to cast to it, come what may. Better not to wade unless it is absolutely essential to reach a lie or a fish which could not be covered because of distance or movement of the fly.

Wading can be dangerous and great care is required to retain stability and, more important, to avoid splashing and shock waves which disturb fish and make the difference between a good rise and a short rise. Fish appear to distinguish between these waves and the rings from another's jump; they may see quite far under water, and one disturbed fish can disturb others which might take.

It is wise to stand with feet apart, sideways to the stream and never back to it. Wade quietly by feel and have one foot secure before the other is moved. Do not become fixed to one spot: as on the bank, keep moving on out of consideration for fellow anglers who may be coming down after you, on either your own bank or the other. And do not become so engrossed that you wade too deep, or edge downstream on a bank, with deep on either side and no way onwards — returning against the current can give some very anxious moments. A few minutes' care in looking at the pool bottom before you wade may prevent a lot of sorrow later. There is good advice in other writings on what to do if you fall in: I cannot swim but there's nothing I shirk, though I do take care. Occasionally my familiarity brings a stumble which reminds me of the greater care needed as the years go by and acuteness of judgement goes with them.

Shelving rocks and boulders can be hazardous to wade on and among, but the danger is so obvious it maintains alertness. A shelving bank of sand or small shingle can be treacherous: it may give way and pull you down, even if you do not appear to be right on the edge of it; you can see it in daylight and judge your distance, but, at dusk, extra care is needed. I was once wading across a river in a deep fast glide, just above the rush down to the next pool. It was a shingle bottom but just too deep for me and my feet came off it. Somehow, I kept upright and managed to bounce on the bottom as I was carried down. Luckily there was no stone to trip me before I bobbed into shallower, though faster water and was wading again. Maybe it was as well I did not have waders on and was naturally athletic, otherwise I could have been in real trouble.

The use of a short rod — one too short for the job — tempts us to wade sometimes. Water seems to draw me on, particularly if waders are being worn. A step or two, over the ankles, is almost irresistible. But try not to wander in too far and disturb the lies. It is often better to keep as far back as one can.

A wading stick is a most comforting support and no bother to carry and use. The feel of a fish on the end of your line as you wade ashore can divide your powers of concentration, and the aid of a staff could be especially welcome.

It may be that to approach a salmon head on is less obvious than from the side, but its sense of smell or taste may come into use. Some years ago, there were reports of salmon having stopped running a fish-pass when men were wading in and working at the top of it, far out of sight and where any diversion of the current could not have any effect. When the men came out the fish ran. This was tried many times and appeared to be a fact. The smell or taste seems to have been treated as a danger signal by fish already wary of a new route. I have before me now, in 1977, a report from University of Wisconsin scientists that they have identified (from data derived from two separate field studies) the Coho salmon's process of homing by smell. The Atlantic salmon may be no different: wary when in a lie, but careless on a free run. On occasions whilst wading I have seen them pass close by. It may not be vital information for the wader but worth bearing in mind — as is having a change of clothing in the car!

8
Disturbance of Fish

It may be that salmon do not need sleep as we know it, but they do appear to have inactive times every day and these vary during the year. We are sure they are all asleep sometimes! Nevertheless, it is more than an amusing remark, and deserves the serious attention now being given by scientists.

Indeed, fish can be most lethargic, and there are suggestions by a number of anglers that stoning a pool, putting a dog through it, having a swim oneself in it, or some other artistic manner of stirring up the place, arouses those that dose. No doubt it does, but to awaken is different from to frighten. I have yet to see any evidence that such activities arouse fish to take, and I believe it a foolish fallacy. It is possible that a fresh fish could come into the pool and take, or some remote lie could be left undisturbed and produce a fish. There is reward for treating a fish with some respect and assuming it has a sense of self-protection in a fairly high degree, though, at times, it can act with unbelievable stupidity, but don't we all!

First over a short pool with a properly presented fly will kill more fish than second down. Whether this is due to readily-taking fish accepting the first offer, or to the disturbance putting others off, does not matter. I have never found fishing down a pool a second time more successful except when I have made a change of fly or technique. A spinner through a pool destroys it for the fly man, and fly should go down it first, no matter which bank. I do not want to step into the purist controversy over fly-only fishing: it does not arise here, where the reference is merely to disturbance. The bigger the river and the higher the water level, the less the ill effects. It is etiquette. Fly before spinner does not irritate anyone.

Spinner before fly does, whichever bank you are on. So let us all try to keep us all happy. The number of anglers is increasing rapidly and there is great pressure on water worth fishing, so we must give a care for each other.

There is no doubt that, once fish have become static in a lie, the more they are cast over, the less likely are they to take; they need a long rest before they will. The effect seems to be cumulative and the more the disturbance, the greater the effect, even if there is a day between each of the repeated upsets. Trolling with an outboard engine, or with oars, in shallow water will ruin the fly fishing for the day and, if done repeatedly, the fish will not take until they have moved quite voluntarily to another lie. The staler the fish, the more sensitive it is. A fresh fish can move into the disturbed lie and take, but this does not affect the issue. A disturbed fish needs a rest before it will show interest in a fly again and will respond more to a fine presentation than a heavy one.

It is quite a common sight in low water in a loch suddenly to see many fish jumping and plunging not far from the boat after it has crossed a deepening where there is a lie. The fish spray out from it in their wild rush to escape from danger. It is not a 'day rise'. It was a disturbance. It is so on a river, too, whatever form the disturbance may take.

It is of great importance to give serious thought to the dangers of unsettling fish. A walk along the bank of a pool yet to be fished, with rod high and shadow from the sun behind thrown far across, is enough to put a fish off. I have been well rewarded for taking such care. I take a boat upwind past a drift, rowing or with out-board engine, so that the wash does not reach out to the lies. An angler on the famous Grimersta fishing in Lewis wrote how extremely quietly and gently the senior ghillie rowed to a favourite gathering place of fish, without disturbing them — and that, mark you, in waters with an abundance of fish. So how much more important to take care when there are but few fish around, as in so many places!

Fishing is essentially a quiet sport, not that I believe talking is heard in some form by fish, though it may be so. But many are angling as an escape from business or chatter elsewhere. This great form of rehabilitation can only come from peaceful concentration on the art.

The use of polaroid lenses may deceive us into approaching too close. Alarming vibrations are carried out by the water to fish from many sources — walking heavily on a peaty bank which goes right to the water's edge, rocking a boat and sending out shock waves. This is all too easy to do without being aware of it, as when standing up, rocking with each cast of a short rod, the clumsy use and thump of oars in rowlocks or thole pins, knocks in the boat. All can send the 'danger around' signals to fish. Shingle absorbs the shock waves and, though noisy to the walker, they do not seem to be transmitted out to the water.

It is better to be over-cautious rather than risk disturbing perhaps the only fish which might take. This is one reason why a good fisherman can make the most of his chances in terms of fish caught. Other causes of disturbance are mentioned in other pages, and not repeated here.

Records are always sought, personal and territorial, but full enjoyment is not necessarily measured by numbers and weights — more by satisfaction in achievement. Both can come by a quiet respectful approach to the great adventure of fishing for salmon.

9
The Ghillie

The name means a boy or a lad, and the accepted Gaelic spelling is 'gillie'. There is a marked difference between the stalking gillie and the fishing ghillie and I write of the latter only.

The old-time ghillie was a man of great character with a wide knowledge of nature and, indeed, of much else, since he was an avid reader. I knew many of them — steeped in tradition, easy going, but by no means simple; often appearing to be deep in thought, but whether thinking or making an impression I was not always sure. To befriend one, and fish with him, was an education and a memorable experience. Never servile but always courteous, they had a quiet confidence and patience in dealing with difficult beings and situations. There are still a few around, and not all of them are old.

The ghillie was the one reluctant to go home at the end of the day, or to give up when conditions meant little hope of a fish. He was anxious to have the best catch of the day. In circles that mattered, his name was the one linked with the catch. Many never spared the angler who persistently missed fish. If he could not show disapproval outright, he let it show in undertones. A ghillie's disapproval was not to be taken lightly by an angler, when real character was behind it. The ghillie was the 'boss', and is today: and, perhaps like many bosses, he must be humoured.

In so many ways a good ghillie is worth much more than his pay and his dram. He is a gem, never a slouch, and there are too few of them. No fear of setting out without some item of equipment. He may not bother much with the flies you have; he usually has his own 'killers'. Clothing and food are not forgotten, but he may silently consider the need to mention the refreshments so essential to the day. He will assemble tackle, but knots are not generally accepted as his responsibility except with the inexperienced, the completely trusting, and those who obviously need help, without admitting it!

He is quick to assess the angler's skill or lack of it. Some are distinctly reluctant to voice approval of one's best efforts; the whimsical expression in the eyes may suggest it has all been done before — and better! He takes time to make a decision about you but, if you do win through, it is glory indeed. One ghillie's philosophy was summed up by saying of a salmon, 'When he wants it, he'll have it!' Credit is hard to come by.

The story goes that an onlooker mentioned to a ghillie that his guest, who was fishing the pool in front of them, did not seem to have a fly on his cast and he thought that he, the ghillie, should tell him and put on another fly. 'Ach,' said the weary old boy, 'he'll no catch onything onyway!'

At the start of a day he can paint a picture of vast numbers of voracious fish 'just achin' to get at your fly'. In a bad spell, he will always find portents of good fortune — the river to rise or fall, the light to change, or tides to be good and fish due in — all to keep up a sagging enthusiasm in one who may have only a fortnight's fishing each year. Nothing is too much trouble if it might add to the pleasure of an appreciative sportsman. Some great fellows have a delightful way of addressing the angler (always 'yourself') in the third person, and speaking of you as 'himself'.

Some are good fishermen, but one who is first-class on the oars and who knows the lies in lochs and rivers is more valuable. On a loch, the length of the boat inshore or out may be the difference between success and failure. What an asset to be shown the exact lies at all heights of water, where to wade and where to stand, and the way from pool to pool without endless mountaineering, fights through bushes, detours of bogs and climbs over fences. His knowledge may be limited to a few rivers and lochs in a small area, but he knows the water in all its moods and, it would seem at times, the very fish.

The fly or bait to be used is the currently successful one, albeit a 'secret' from brother ghillies. The best way of fishing the stretch is adopted from the start, and not a lie is missed. He is anxious that you catch fish but, willing though he may be to stay, he must not be kept out too long. Many ghillies are quite selfless in the quest for fish, but they may not assess your fishing ability as highly as you do! Moreover, he is doing a job, and overtime comes into the reckoning at the end of the day.

Some ghillies are surly, bored-looking, critical and intolerant of your wasting good fishing when it may be a struggle to hold the boat in a strong wind and big waves. Some are short of words and with little time to spend over the poor stretches. Such a man may rush you, but he will have you casting over fish. A good angler of similar outlook with catch a lot of fish. The average angler fishes hard but not restively, and wants a peaceful day with reasonable success, instead of a hectic challenge. The less tolerant ghillie is not the kind to have teach a beginner of less than the toughest fibre, but he is of great help in advising on the lies.

One or two ghillies have a horror of getting their feet wet. And there are anglers who expect the ghillie to go in waist deep to gaff or net a fish! If the fish is brought in properly, there will be no mistakes with net or gaff or hand. And no need for wet feet. Some trout netters use the net most efficiently in the manner of a bludgeon, but this is not recommended when dealing with a salmon. I know some experienced fishers and ghillies who still let their excitement verge on the uncontrollable. They never make a mistake, though I feel they live dangerously.

I remember being with a famous tournament caster on the Spey. He was wading up to his middle only three feet out from the bank. I do not know why he was in the water at all — probably a compulsive wader. He hooked a fish and, almost immediately, started shouting at me to gaff it. An astonishing reaction from one with such wide experience. I was not prepared to reach out at any time, stick in the gaff, and perhaps follow the fish in a headlong plunge — or miss it! There was a lovely beach nearby, and gaffing was unnecessary. I got another to pick up the gaff and, after much slipping and splashing and bad language, with the fish lying on its side on the shingle, the gaff was eventually scraped into it and the episode was over. Fun to watch, but a poor display of what to do.

Some students on holiday make excellent ghillies. They may fish a bit, but this is unimportant if they are good oarsmen. They do not have long experience of the water but they have good memories, soon know the main lies, and are a joy to be out with. The angler does not need to worry about rowing, keeping the boat on the drift, or the way to the pools or the boundaries, and he can exercise his

own water lore with a feeling of hopeful co-operation rather than a
weary resignation.

Other ghillies we know — never far from home and always
heading there for 5 p.m., with fish definitely 'off the rise', or with
complete disregard of fish being 'on the rise'. Maybe my own
training was a bit hard when, on many occasions, I had to set out at
7.30 a.m., row about four miles, meet my guests at 9 a.m., ghillie
and handle the boat until 6 p.m. when they would go home. Left
with the four miles row to the boathouse at Rhu Noa on Loch
Maree, I usually fished the good spots. But the pay was good —
37½p per day. Laws and fishery regulations prevent such as this
happening now. In those days too, outboard engines were not
allowed on the loch, a wise management decision as may be seen
now, years after their introduction and indiscriminate use.

There are few who take up the life of the full-time ghillie now. It
is a seasonable job and there are many other attractions. Yet some
continue to make a life of it, a calling such as the old type had, with
little financial reward but with great satisfaction to themselves and
joy to those who have days with them. We cannot expect men to
make the financial sacrifice necessary just to please us, and we must
pay for the privilege of having them available. Similar changes
have come to hotel life, where in a family hotel the guest got the
best that could be given for little cost, and with no thought of the
work involved. Cutting the service was a disaster, but the guest
was unwilling to pay the cost of retaining it. Let's look after our
ghillies and keep the standard high.

Bob who rang the church bell every Sabbath was of great
interest. He was getting on in years and had the long slow heather
stride of a man who had walked the hills and river banks since
boyhood. A heavy moustache and a well-proportioned pipe, as
well perhaps as his deliberate speech, made him seem older than he
was. He was a good fisher, a discreet poacher, and always in
demand by fishermen friends and guests of long standing. Bob
knew the times when a dozen or more ghillies would turn up at the
hotel each morning but perhaps only half would be engaged for the
day. A good man reaped the reward of sure employment and Bob
knew all the salmon lies in the rivers and lochs, and all the lochs
with good trout. A serious fellow on the Sabbath, he would ring
the bell and close the church doors at the start of the service, then
return with all due solemnity to sit at the end of the pew — on one

occasion, close to a friend of mine. At the first need for spectacles, he opened his case and there, exposed with them, were some salmon flies and a fly size chart. He closed the case quickly and quietly, but the two men's eyes met and the youthful twinkle in Bob's eyes spoke volumes!

It was this same worthy who was ghillie to a big tough Scots Canadian 'home' on holiday. His chauffeur warned me not to give the Canadian any alcoholic drink, and experience taught me to heed such counsel. However, towards mid-week he begged a bottle of rum 'to give to Bob's wife'. He took it to her but, two nights later, instead of coming to the hotel for dinner, he visited Bob's home, asked for the rum and a glass, and proceeded to drink the lot himself! What an experience for a man such as Bob, who enjoyed a dram occasionally. The Canadian returned to the hotel at 2 a.m., made a lot of noise and caused me much concern. I tried to sedate him with a glass and a bottle of whisky but it did not produce the desired effect. Hours later I got him to his car, headed South to better fishing! As a parting gesture, with a hand on my shoulder and 'I couldn't do a thing like that to you, Mac', he produced a bundle of hotel cutlery from his pocket!

More than fifty years ago my father came in one evening with a broad smile. He had just been talking to an old fellow who had ghillied all his life, always a happy meeting. I remember the old ghillie well. He was nearing eighty, and one of the old school. 'Speerish' is the phonetical spelling of his nickname, but I do not know its meaning nor do I know his real name. A large birch tree on a point of the loch was named after him, and I was sad when it was wantonly cut down during some road works. Off that point was a lie of salmon and, further out in the deeper water, seatrout. When we first met Speerish, he told my father how he was failing and got severe pains at times but, if he was careful and had a good drop of whisky when the pains came on he was all right. Otherwise he would be very bad for days. Just then he doubled up in pain — and got his whisky!

The local men know the fishing and get the fish, but one ghillie who has a great reputation as a fisher takes his knowledge a step further. He usually gets a fish just as soon as he is handed the rod. Many fishers give him a few casts after long dull spells, — sometimes planned dull spells I suspect! The offer is not taken up at poor spots, but talk is directed to produce the offer at the right time. 'That's the end of the drift' or 'We're past the best of it now, but I'll just have a cast for luck.' And bang — a fish — as expected in such a·good lie! I know that game! The poor fisher is liable to suffer most in this way. Entries in many fishing registers over many years show catches which would have been insignificant but for this ghillie's contributions.

On the other hand, I have known those who were almost devoid of fishing knowledge, with no interest in fishing themselves, but who kept the boat well, did all that was required by the river, and come what may, inspired a hope of fish so great that the angler enjoyed his every day with never a hint of despondency. What more do we need in a ghillie?

Fly charts which relate all geographic variables to fly size are being developed, and they will aid the fisher in his choice of fly. But they will never replace the advice of the true ghillie. Bless him.

10
Other than Fly

Worthwhile fishing is not available to all, and many have no way of learning how to cast a fly and fish it. But a fixed spool reel is easy to use; a spinning rod and lures are cheap. The sport can be tried out without any great expense or loss even if not enjoyed. And success is more likely for the beginner than with fly. Sometimes water is too high, too coloured or too cold for other than some form of bait to be used.

The fly fisherman — purist or not — must remember these things and know that most forms of spinning and bait fishing demand great skill. I do not wish to go into the details of tackle used, with diagrams of worms impaled on hooks or the like, or of the methods of using them. However, I would like to mention some of them, and perhaps show a little why I prefer fly and recommend fly to everyone I teach.

Probably the lowest forms are trolling on a loch or harling on a river, but I do not condemn these completely. There are people who would not have any sport at all if they did not do one or the other — the unduly incapacitated or those quite unable to master the art of casting even a spinner. The fun and excitement of playing a fish are theirs and they can talk of it long after. The hooking of the fish is in the hands of the man at the oars or, alas nowadays, at the helm of an outboard engine. There is skill in the choice and mounting of a sprat of the right size — cut or whole — and in the selection of spinner. The lure must be brought past the fish at the right speed and depth to induce it to take. The depth can be controlled by the weight on the tackle, the length of the line out and the rate at which the boat is travelling. A bait swinging in a curve can be especially effective. Trolling can be good fun when alone —

with two rods and a 'poker' out. Many skills — and some courage sometimes — are needed when a fish is hooked.

Many lochs are famed for the fish they give to trolled baits and spinners. In bygone days this may not have had any effect on the early runs but it could now, with so few fish in them; these early fish might be of great value to the whole system if left to breed, as one must assume that early fish produce early fish.The numbers caught may reflect the numbers running the rivers. They take well in rivers if the water temperature is low and they are not running straight through, to be caught in the lochs above. In these days of depleted stocks they might be protected a little more by delaying the opening date for trolling, or banning it altogether, at least until stocks are built up again. Fish will take a fly in a loch in colder water than many admit — particularly if not disturbed by trolls. As with rivers, fishing fly calls for greater skill and harder work than spinning, in casting and keeping a boat to obtain results. It is no argument against fly to say a large fly is just like a sprat or spinner. If so, why not just use it?

A spinner may be cast long distances by an inactive person, from a seat in a boat or on a bank. A fixed spool reel is easy to use in all weather conditions.

A great variety of baits and spinners is used: sprats, prawns, shrimps, worms and spoons are a few, and all call for great skill in successful use.

Reference is made elsewhere to delicacy in fly presentation in low water, yet, when small and fine seems the order of the day, I get fish on large flies. Fly is often better than a spinner and may well produce more fish over the year to an angler equally good at both.

Before World War II, and, indeed, during it, I had ample opportunity to fish parr tail and I often did so experimentally, because I never ceased to be astonished at the response of fish in a shallow stream even on a clear day. A parr, cut obliquely and on a tackle to make it spin in a circular wobble — not tightly as with a Devon minnow — looked a bit like a shark bait as it spun across. It seemed irresistible. The risk of a £5 fine for killing the parr was not a deterrent. I condemn the method without reservation. A small trout is not effective. I refer to it only out of interest in the reaction of a salmon to it when fished as it should be. I was taught this technique but I shall not teach anyone. I do not fear any upsurge of such fishing: it is difficult, with many seemingly insurmountable snags. It may now be a dead method, only vaguely remembered.

One pool I fished every March held fish which took a long time to take a prawn. They had to see it many times before they responded: surely fish I would never have caught in that pool on a fly, but later might have caught upstream on fly.

When worming, a lead is needed to get the bunch of worms down to the bottom and bump along downstream for good results. And how easy to mistake the 'rug' of an eel for a fish.

Any tackle sunk in legitimate technique can be too easily adapted to illegal fishing. Fish may be foul-hooked intentionally, or quite accidentally. It is better to try to reduce risks than leave such a wide open door to shady methods. The water can be destroyed for the fly fisherman: it may be lost to a club or association by termination of the lease, if unworthy tactics are used by any member. A 'Fly Fishing Only' rule would seem a solution to the problems of making the maximum amount of fishing available to the true sportsmen in some areas. Perhaps there is a little of the poacher in us all. And maybe a good spirit to have, if not a greedy one; there is so much more to sport than making it pay its way. Making the sport at least contribute to the cost is the only way some can afford it. It is an added satisfaction, with no dangers if using fly only, but the heavy tubes and heavy lines used on some rivers leave a lot to be desired.

A foul-hooked fish should be returned — a good rule to enforce on all. I had a pupil not so many years ago whose first fish was foul-hooked. I had told him the law, as I do with everyone. He returned it. I confess I felt desperately sorry, but he was unperturbed; others ribbed him, but he did not mind — a true sport and not a stupid one. I hope he is rewarded with a life of great pleasure in fishing.

A few years ago, on our first summer holiday together, my wife and I went to Norway. I paid my rent in advance — £70 for one rod for a week's fishing on the river Driva. Expensive, but a once only event. I wanted fly fishing and could have this on three pools. On arrival, I found only one pool could be fished with any likelihood of success from my bank, and, on it and the bank opposite, there were ten others fishing — all spinning or using worm or prawn. It went on day and night. Fires were lit and rods, at the ready, stacked nearby, like rifles with fixed bayonets. Fishing down the pool was a dangerous venture — one ounce and one and a half ounce spoons and other curiously shaped articles hurled to and fro under uncertain control and too close for comfort. Dusk brought little relief, except that I could only hear the things whistle through the air — to stop with a splash of relief! But for that excellent fisher, Johan Johansen from Oslo, known as the 'Salmon King' when he is fishing the June runs, my week would have been ruined. He tried to sort out some of the others of various nationalities devoid of any English. They caught only one fish, and the poor results may have helped to thin them out. In addition to the one salmon, they had some small seatrout. My wife Barbara fished for only five minutes and caught one salmon. I had three more and twenty-five seatrout up to seven pounds — all on fly. We would have had tremendous fishing but for the opposition. They merely cast out and wound in, without any sign that they knew what their bait was doing; some asked for instruction, but I was on holiday! They had their pleasure, I suppose, and there were plenty to take my place. But what a waste of marvellous fishing! Nevertheless, I would go back gladly, but for the cost. The snow-specked mountains formed the valley of the river, and fishing from the first signs of daybreak until almost sunrise was a fine experience.

I am fortunate in having known many of the great fishings in former years, when signs of disturbance were seen perhaps more readily than nowadays. I suppose it is only natural that the more harried they are, the more wary the fish become — and the more care we must take.

Some other time I may enlarge on trolling, spinning and bait fishing — there are great skills in them. I have had the luck to fish most ways and to learn many of these skills. But I remain firmly on the side of those who wish to have rules and areas clearly defined — fly only and, if you will, spinning only. It is because of our limited fishing and a great concern for it that I feel that there must be a reduction in spinning to ensure that the maximum number of anglers may enjoy salmon fishing and become better anglers. A golfer is not content with using a putter only: he must learn the rest of the game. So must the angler his sport!

11
Courtesies

There is such a demand for fishing on lochs and rivers that it is all too easy for a few to spoil the sport for many. This is seldom intentional and, in most cases, is due entirely to an ignorance of etiquette in fishing and not to a lack of sportsmanship. Courtesy costs nothing, so let's consider some unwritten laws and seek to obey them.

When there is a rod on a pool, whether on your own bank or the other, let it fish down a considerable distance, well below where your fly will swing round, before starting at the neck. The longer you can delay your start, the more rest the pool is having. If others are waiting, you have to follow down sooner than you care. Fish along reasonably quickly at, say, two casts every three steps. If you rise a fish, rest it for a minute or two and try again, but do not become like a heron and stay long on the spot. A fellow angler will not harass you and will gladly give you the little extra time. If there are other pools, he will probably leave you to it — a good principle, rise or not.

The number of rods on a beat is usually strictly controlled and there is no overcrowding. On some rivers there is no restriction on the number of rods which might appear and a voluntary queue system is necessary. This must be observed strictly. Rentals are high, and some proprietors allow rather many rods on a beat.

Fly should have priority over bait, but this may well depend on your time of arrival and the spinner there before you. Many fishings have 'fly only' stretches and areas where spinning is allowed: so, there is no confusion in this good arrangement.

You may want to stay at a pool, or at a drift, for a long time: by all means do so, but allow others to fish through if they wish. Do not try to claim the water for your own exclusive use: this is done all too often and can lead to friction and harsh words.

When walking along, keep as far back from the side as need be to avoid disturbance. If the bank is high, do not be silhouetted against the sky, and keep the rod low to prevent a shadow being cast across the water. And keep the rod tip to the rear, for its own safety! The bank may be a good conductor of vibration, so do not thump along with each step. Keep wading under control and avoid all forms of disturbance of fish, out of consideration for others as well as for your own benefit. A rod which upsets the accepted conventions of a fishing may not be allowed on it again.

As mentioned elsewhere, anglers are mostly a friendly lot and one of their great joys is the escape from everyday work and cares, and from endless chatter. A word of greeting is fine, but if your company is wanted it will be quite evident. Uninvited talk is seldom welcome and, least of all, by the waterside. This is an aspect of fishing which should be kept for other times, over a drink or in winter time when memories and discussions keep us in tune for fishing in days to come. Leave the fisher to his contest with the fish in uninterrupted earnestness and concentration. Many fear being thought selfish by wishing for peace or, even, solitude when fishing. There is no need, for this kind of fishing is not a gregarious sport.

When watching a fish being played, keep well away and do not be a distraction. Any help wanted will be called for. In giving assistance, do exactly as asked; most know what they want done, be it right or wrong in your opinion, and it is better they remain responsible for the capture or loss of the fish.

Keep clear of the back cast so that you are neither in the way of the caster nor hooked by him. Do not go too close to any pool to see if there are fish in lies. I have found some water bailiffs very careless and not at all considerate in their approach. Perhaps some are appointed because of their brawn rather than their knowledge of fishing.

Do not take a boat, by oar or engine, in front of another on a drift or on any fishable water. Normally a 'drift' is from one main point forming a bay to the other. It is in order to go in and start at a point unless another boat is too close to it. This is not permissible at points along a recognised and, usually, named drift. Salmon are noted for their specific lies, in a deepening or by a rock or bank of weeds. It is not often that they are caught elsewhere. The boat can be held back so that the lies can be fished properly but not allowed to cross and disturb them. But do not try to 'hog' the spot; treat it as you would in a pool or stream. It is good policy that so many waters are now split up into beats, with a limited number of rods or boats on each. The water is fished more thoroughly and there is little likelihood of irritation between anglers. Remember, opinions are varied and wide, and annoyance can arise from the other having 'unreasonable' views. So play safe. When sharing a boat, fish your own 'beat' from it only; should the boat 'run' in your direction, allowing you to fish all the water first, shorten your line. You will cover plenty of water and still leave fresh territory for the rod following.

Unless the water is out of order for fly, do not spin it: bait or spinner spoil the water for the fly fisher. The spinner may well be down the pool before fly has a chance — from either bank. In high water it does not matter much but, in low, it does. The rules are clear on most fishings but, on others, you are left to decide on fly or spinner or leave it for somewhere else.

I do not scorn bait fishing. I know the skills called for from a bait angler are great, but the vast majority spin because it is easier than casting a fly sufficiently well to catch some fish. This is surely a fact. Fly gives less disturbance and a better chance for all and, I believe, it yields a greater number of fish for the angler equally skilled at fly or bait. I relate in another chapter my experience in having my fly fishing compete with all forms of bait — worm, prawn, spoons, sprats and some bits of metal I could not identify!

I hope all waters will have clear rules before long, so that each can enjoy his form of the sport to the full without fear of offending another. To be first over a beat in early morning is fair play, but some lochs and rivers come under rules which restrict the hours of fishing and where the less active do not have to compete with the early risers, or those coming off early work shifts.

Although catching fish is the aim, for most, it is not all of fishing. The use of bait or spinner does not necessarily produce fish but, alas, it opens the door to other methods which may be illegal.

One river I know does not permit the use of a cast with three flies on it because there are three hooks. This is taking things a little too far but, while a rule, it must be accepted. Rentals are high and have to be accepted without undue worry about catching enough to pay it, lest there be temptations to 'fetch' fish which will not come of their own free will — and sport forgotten. Few fishings are worth the rent asked, if judged by the number of fish caught, but in beautiful surroundings and only the sounds of nature breaking the peace, the value to the true sportsman cannot be assessed, and he pays what he must for it.

Wherever you fish, ensure that your permit is in order, that you know all the regulations, that you are on the right beat or taking the right boat. There is no scope for error in this. A good fishing must be under strict control to keep it so. The left bank of a river is the left bank as you look downstream.

Close gates, do not cross fences except at specific places. Keep clear of crops and do not light fires. Be anti-litter-minded about all waste — especially nylon, which can cause so much suffering to birds and animals. The excitement of fishing is great but give a thought to the countryside and its life. It contributes so much towards the pleasures of a day's fishing. And the experienced must gently guide the ways of the beginner or the ignorant.

12

Intuition

It has been accepted by some zoologists for some time that fish are not colour blind and that they have their delights and dislikes in colour. No doubt it is the degree to which the colour shows up in the water that attracts fish. The human eye sees objects and colour underwater, but this does not indicate the fish's response and it may be very different from the human response. Yellow appears to show up better than red, and this may partly explain why a yellow fly or golden sprat yields results in the cold water of Spring and a reddish fly or prawn does better later in the season. But the jet black fly does well in the cold water and the large red and black fly too! To use a bright fly on a bright day and a dark one on a dull day is a good old general guide. I cannot identify in detail what tempts the fish to take under the greatly differing conditions we meet in a season: size of fly is of primary importance, but colour affects the choice of size and I have found through trial on many rivers that a Green Highlander, size one, appears equivalent to a Black Doctor or Jock Scott size 2/0. The subject calls for research and experiment. My own choice of fly is governed by its appearance in the water. I have an indefinable feeling — perhaps an affinity towards fish — which is VERY important to my success. This attitude of mind derives from an accumulation of experience and helps to pinpoint the right choice. I do not fish mechanically, in blind hope or trusting to luck: I make a considered judgement and expect success. I cast with a purpose, and although a fish may take when you relax or look away, I do not believe it can sense the dangerous intent in your eye!

Salmon are not as capricious as some would have us believe. It is easy to see what agrees with one's own preconceived ideas. Failures are fewer for the systematic angler who has made accurate observations and has all his knowledge readily at hand. The novice tends to rush in with theories on flimsy evidence, or is content to cover up all by talk of the capriciousness of the salmon, or quote from 'A Book of Angling' written by Francis Francis in 1872 — 'Depend upon it brother angler that there is no dogmatic rule to be laid down either for maidens or fish'!

In 1938, Chalmers wrote in his book 'Salmon Fishing in Little Rivers' — 'In every fishing circle there is always one man who has the reputation of catching more fish than the others and the envy with which he is regarded sometimes leads alas to a suspicion of his methods'. A man who knows the water and the lies does not waste casts or time, and he gets the fish.

The controversy over the colour of fly lines goes on unresolved with good arguments on all sides. A white line seems conspicuous to me. It may show up well to a fish when cast against a dark background, and I prefer a dark one purely for my own peace of mind. When ill-used, a line of any colour can disturb fish. The leader thickness is of much more importance and, in any case, I prefer to offer the fly to the fish before the line goes near it: colour is relatively unimportant to me. A white or light-coloured line is of great help to many in casting and in locating the fly: they should use one.

Whatever the colour of the line or the cost of it, tackety (hobnail) boots can make mincemeat of it as it falls loose on the stones when handlining.

I have referred elsewhere to the use of short rods when I feel long ones are appropriate. I used to have a great yearning to use a short light rod but a varied experience helped me to grow out of it. So many anglers came fitted out by some fine firm in London, with beautiful rods, reels and lines, and primed to use them mainly for seatrout but often for salmon too. Fish rose short and were not hooked because of bad light or some ill wind, but never because of unsuitable equipment or technique. It is not the distance cast which matters so much as the fishing of the fly thereafter.

A short rod and heavy line, with which casting is so easy, does not allow for good control of the fly or sensitive contact with it. The effective use of the dropper on loch or river is wellnigh impossible. A longish rod, of twelve feet or so, is ideal for seatrout or salmon in conditions when fine tackle is advisable. A light line is easy to cast after a little practice: the delightful twelve-footer Sharpe's make for me is perfect with a number two Kingfisher line (A.F.T.M. 5). The light line means a long line outside the point of the rod to give the right weight for good casting, and a firmer and slower action is required. With a heavy line a comparatively short length is needed to give this weight. I shoot line in my back cast to give the correct weight for a good forward cast. This requires practice, but it is such a worthwhile skill in all fly casting that the effort is well rewarded. I advise the use of a line three grades less than that recommended for the rod for anyone really willing to practise and improve his casting ability. Timing of all the actions must be accurate, and the outcome is most satisfying and, indeed, impressive to see. Many rod makers recommend a line much too heavy for the rod. The heavy line is a flattering aid to the caster and, perhaps, to those rods which need a heavy line to produce some degree of action. But their range of use in fishing is limited.

Recently, an angler with a new fourteen-foot carbon fibre rod had occasion to ask me about a difficulty she had in casting. The line was a very heavy one and I suggested and demonstrated how much better a light one was. She felt aggrieved because the line was recommended with the very expensive outfit, and a selling point was that the rod could be used with a great range of line sizes. It seems to me from some experiences of this kind that purchasers of fine tackle may need more competent guidance than is often given. Having bought such a rod, you cannot but try to convince yourself and others how good it is, though your view may then be a little biased!

Rods do work well with different sizes of line but different casting techniques are necessary. I use my fourteen-foot spliced split cane rod with lines ranging from number six Kingfisher (A.F.T.M. 10) to a number three Kingfisher (A.F.T.M. 6), depending on the demands of the fishing conditions.

It is suggested somewhere that the line should be chosen before the rod. I have sought sound reasons for this order of events but, as yet, have found none. I do not recommend it within the scope of the fishing I discuss in this book. It is wise to sift carefully all the advice you receive so that you do not end up coping with other people's mistaken ideas.

The late Joe Brooks, a great friend from Virginia, was a marvellous angler with world-wide experience. This can be shared by reading his delightful books, 'Trout Fishing' and 'A World of Fishing'. He had a passion for the short rod and though he had some sharp practical lessons on its limited use in Norway and Scotland, he did not change his views. He was angling adviser to ABC TV and he arranged what promised to be a great experience on the Spey when we were to demonstrate our techniques before the cameras — his short rod, my long one. Fees were agreed, reliefs arranged and the prospects were tremendous, but to my greatest disappointment in the world of angling, a bout of infective hepatitis forced me to call off a few days before. The programme was cancelled at considerable cost and, as is the way with such things, the opportunity was lost. It was left to Bing Crosby to make a salmon fishing film on the Derwent, a film of interest but little substance.

Later, I took part in a BBC film. The long rod was used for the hypersensitive seatrout on days bright and calm. Boats were rocked and the water slashed with branches to simulate the effects of a breeze! I willed a fish to take if ever I did! I rose and missed a three-pounder in the still water. Camera and recording boats were called in and I caught the fish! It was played to allow the camera boat to weave in between me and the fish. All fun but rather unprofessional! A fish caught in near impossible conditions. But I feel the strong will to catch that fish even now. Just as I fish for the bigger fish in a pool where my late brother, a fine fisher, would catch the smaller one.

Be intent and mindful of what you do when you are fishing.

13
The Changing Scene

There has been wide speculation as to whether or not the runs of fish are becoming later. In my own time, I have noted a great reduction in the catches from several areas and all for apparently different reasons. Weather conditions, disease at various stages, numbers of predators and netting can produce considerable variations in the figures and have incalculable long-term effects. I accept there is a drop in landings of Spring fish and an increase in grilse in many places.

Before any of the schemes for producing electricity brought disaster, the Perthshire Garry was a fine river which gave fish far above Struan. My father had many fish from it sixty or so years ago in Spring. The earliest was on 17th January, from the Boat Pool, but few were caught above the Pass of Killiecrankie until March. In 1926 or so, the Grampian Scheme diverted water and practically no fish were caught between Tummel Bridge and close to Rannoch Station for a time after the power station was built. My folks had the Tummel Bridge Hotel for a few years, when the Tummel there was a good salmon and grilse river, but left for the North at the earliest signs of this scheme.

The water was diverted from Loch Garry to Rannoch and the high reaches of the river Garry were almost dried up. I fished again for two whole seasons towards the end of the war. There were no fish in February but good fishing mostly in the Pass in March and April, and later, right up to Struan; many of these fish were between twenty and thirty pounds. The power station at Pitlochry was built and yet more water taken, from the tributaries this time. A barrier was put across the river, at its junction with the river Errochtie, to prevent fish going up to and beyond the Falls of

Struan. The vast areas of good spawning in the head waters of the Tummel and the Garry were lost, the Spring fish were gone and, no doubt, this showed in the numbers of Spring fish caught by net and rod on the Tay. The Hydro Board has done great work in restoring runs of fish to what is left of the Garry and the river Tilt, and it will be a very long time, and the end of those hydro-electric schemes, before they will be as of old. There are many hydro schemes and other water extractions in the country, and the total effect on migratory fish must be considerable. We need the schemes and I do not condemn them. I merely wish to mention some of the early effects on fish. There is a limit to what the hydro boards can do. It does not seem to me a good idea to put smolts up into head waters. They may not be good foragers for food and, certainly, through some of the reservoirs and lochs, their passage must present great temptations to hungry trout and pike. This experiment has not yet shown itself as an unqualified success.

Two other rivers I knew well gave occasional fish in February until the late forties but since then only one or, perhaps, two have been caught so early in the year. March yielded quite a few fish. On two occasions, that is on two separate years, I caught the first fish of the season from each on the same day. A third year, I got one in the Northern river and went out to the other, five miles to the South, hoping to repeat the performance yet again. I arrived to find a watcher just losing one! This strengthened my belief that they came on the same tide — and at a high tide. In April, about 1947, I caught twenty-one fish in eight days' fishing in the North river and it was good until mid-May, when there was a lull in the runs of fish until the end of the third week in June. It seemed these early fish could be a source of income to the coastal nets which, incidentally, were controlled by the owner of the rivers. The nets went on and few fish were caught in the river until towards the end of June. In a year or two the early run was so decimated that the nets were taken off. This was before the salmon disease, Ulcerative Dermal Necrosis. The odd fish is being caught now and, no doubt, the run will return. A hatchery is run and salmon fry are poured into the headwaters in thousands every year, but whether these are the progeny of early running fish or not is unknown. I have not seen any evidence anywhere, indicating that stocking prolific salmon rivers does good. It seems to be merely stocking with fry a river already overstocked with fry; food and space are limited. The extra fry might lead to further mortality in the Spring runner fry from the odd early fish which may have spawned on the redds. During this bad spell I was running courses of angling instruction for beginners each April, on the rivers. I asked the owner one day in May if he was having some luck. 'No, your people have frightened all the fish away!' I thought he was joking: he must be, but he wasn't, and he made that quite clear. I wondered who was advising about the management of the fishings.

An East coast river I knew well had once been at its best in February and March. Two marvellous ghillies, great fishermen, now, alas, gone, who had spent most of their lives on the river, agreed (and this in itself was noteworthy) on what had happened. The river came out of a loch and the headwaters were two small rivers from away in the hills which were never fished. Then, in time, they seemed a good source of income and were let for fishing, with no restrictions ever enforced. The pools — one at a small waterfall — were almost cleared of fish each August and September, and these ghillies maintained that the Spring stock was killed off. The Spring runs certainly began to deteriorate soon afterwards. Perhaps drainage of the peat moors led to deposits choking spawning redds and to destruction by short, sharp, high floods. The water level might have become unduly low in dry conditions, and fry lost. It might also support the belief that spring running fish breed spring running fish, that is, that like breeds like. The transfer of fry from one early river to another in an effort to encourage early runs does not seem to have been a success anywhere.

The runs in many areas were almost completely destroyed by the salmon disease UDN. Recovery of the runs is slow, and excessive and indiscriminate netting, without a thought for the future, is making complete recovery unlikely. Salmon now at £4 plus per pound in Spring is a great temptation to take all and let tomorrow look after itself. Some netting authorities do make efforts to adjust their activities to the water level in the rivers but they are able to do so without any ill effect on their pockets: when main runs come in, it matters little which part of the run is taken. In some places — too many in fact — nets and rod fishings are run by completely independent owners and the nets may operate for days on end, picking up any odd fish which may come into the estuary. This is particularly so in the early months of April and May. The angler

would catch a few of them but many would go on to spawn and
their offspring form good runs in a few years' time. It is interesting
to note that, according to returns of fish caught, the ratio of net-
caught to rod-caught in Scotland is seven to one. It is not 'all very
well' for me to say all this. Truly I do not own any net or rod
fishing, nor can I afford to rent them, but I do feel very concerned
for the future of salmon fishing. The agreement about the netting of
fish off the coast of Greenland is good, but our real problems seem
to be around our own shores. Despite all, there are many salmon in
our lochs and rivers to be caught with rod and line.

Spring fish in most Scottish rivers have a sizeable loch on their
course, a safe haven until they move on for spawning. This is true
of many rivers which are long and without waterfalls or great
rapids. Some others with lochs are short, tumbling rivers and never
have had any great runs of Spring fish, say, in February and
March. I recall the good runs we had into a loch (Loch Maree) and
river (Gairbhe) I fished a lot from the early twenties until the start
of the war, mainly towards the end of March, and in April and
May. Only twice did we have fish in February. I am told there are
few fish now but I do not know if the disease took any great toll. I
think not, and it would seem netting at sea, far and near, must take
the blame. Certainly it is primarily a seatrout system, but they are
at a low ebb too. However, with the tremendous spawning areas
there, the seatrout will recover, but slowly.

My family saved many heavy seatrout each year, when large
spates at spawning times let them ascend ditches by the road side,
and other little streams where they could not turn and go down to
deeper burns as the floods receded. Often our clue to their presence
was the sound of splashing in water hidden by rushes. We turned
them and ushered them down to safety, blocking the route they had
just been. It seemed very important, though there were masses of
fish spawning; and perhaps it was. Poachers made frequent forays
on them, but whether for the ova for hatcheries or the fish for
drying and pickling, I never knew. I hope any stocking to try and
restore the salmon population bears in mind that it is primarily a
seatrout reserve, by nature. It is interesting to note that the river
into the loch is formed by two main streams — one from the North
and the other from the South. The latter takes a good number of
salmon and all the seatrout, while the other takes only salmon: no
seatrout run it, though a few spawn in a low tributary. There used

to be good catches of salmon from this river until a waterfall, which held up the fish, was blasted to clear a way for them. Few fish are taken from it now.

I wonder if a change in the times of the runs is really taking place. Or is it that the decrease in the size of some runs and the increase in others makes an apparent change? In times of plenty we may be a little careless in our observations, but in scarcity note every detail and theorise upon it.

14

Fishing Hotels

The ideal fishing hotel would provide the angler with a comfortable bed, plenty of hot water, good drying facilities, abundance of good food available at almost any time of the day or night, a comfortably furnished and well stocked bar — and a host or hostess of tireless mind and never-wilting stamina. All very costly to provide in a small seasonal hotel in a sparsely populated area.

It was more nearly attained in olden days than now, but times have changed and so have the numbers and attitudes of anglers. Today it is very expensive, and fishing is no longer treated as a free amenity and attraction for the guest: accountants and owners do not allow managers to be content with the small profits of the old-time proprietors and tenants.

Just after the First World War my folks had Tummel Bridge Hotel, a place steeped in history. In one window a small pane bore Mendelssohn's signature, but this was lost when the hotel was demolished and rebuilt for other purposes in the mid-twenties. The fine old place stood at the end of the General Wade bridge. At flood levels, the flagstoned kitchen and passages were ankle deep in a steady flow from back door to front and side doors. A bulwark and sandbags did little to prevent it and although the doors of an old Highland Inn were ever open, this did seem a little bit much! Whisky was brought in at proof strength in barrels — what a basis for a fishing hotel! — but reduced to the legal strength for sale to the public. The calls from the excisemen always ended as great affairs — they were thirsty too!

Only the 'toffs' fished there then. The day was nicely timetabled: breakfast at half past eight; lunch at one o'clock; or an elaborate picnic lunch prepared and packed in huge hampers; afternoon tea;

bath, then dinner at eight. There weren't so many of them and they had to be cared for at little reward. Baths had to be filled with hot water carried in pails from a waterboiler downstairs. There was no hot and cold running water in the bedrooms — hot water cans had to be put round at morning call time and before dinner. Wash basins and slop pails were emptied and made shining, drinking glasses polished and ewers and water carafes filled with fresh water during dinner — usually a six-course meal. Staff had long hours, little time off, and little pay. It was so until the last war.

The great Fords, DFPs, Bentleys or Vulcans were imposing at the door, always polished by chauffeurs whose very life they seemed to be.

Occasionally an angler would have an after-dinner cast — a social event, a try-out of some theory, or a demonstration or a projection of some theory or of prowess — for a jolly hour or so. I was 'that little devil in the red jersey' for a time then to a guest — a General Pink — who got 'rises' from well-placed stones I threw from behind the bushes. He never got too close to me, though he was dangerously near at times!

It was here I had a habit of 'setting' my rod wherever I finished fishing. It caught me many trout and, to my disgust, eels. One evening, as darkness fell and we were having our supper, my father and his accomplices in the family asked about my rod. Yes, I had set it as usual. It was a good night and the fish should feed well. I should maybe have a look at it before I went to bed. I went the half mile up river to have a look. Sure enough — a fish — and a big one — I felt it pull in the stream and, in the half light, I caught a glimpse of its golden side as it turned — a moment later I pulled in a kipper! The hateful lot.

Two years after a tragedy in a hotel in the Highlands, we moved North to take over one of the hotels run by the heartbroken proprietor. The details of how eight people died from food poisoning (botulism) are in medical books. A guest who was there at the time, and whom I knew well, recalled how the local doctor wanted to give heavy doses of whisky, in the firm belief that it would save the people. Botulism is almost unheard of now, but there is an antidote in a medical bank in London, ready in the unlikely event of any recurrence.

The hotel is still a marvellous fishing hotel, but with a rule of no fishing after 6 p.m.

Our hotel was a fine place too and it had its own problems. Despite limited fishing, the angling guests were mostly of the old traditional type, but very keen, eager and energetic. Some wanted a 'tousey tea' (high tea) at 6 p.m., then fished until late, to return tired and in need of food and drink before settling down to noisy talk until the wee sma' oors, disturbing other guests. Others wanted to fish early in the morning — a good time under certain conditions. To the fisherman who wanted out about half-past nine in the morning and back before six o'clock, with a good hour's break for lunch, this seemed unfair. He did not come to fish water which was thrashed and disturbed day and night. I understand his views completely: many areas should be fished for comparatively short periods only and given long spells of rest, which seatrout above all must have, to play the game as we know they can. It made great demands on staff as well as mine host, who had to stay sober to survive.

These are attitudes towards fishing which are difficult to mix, and least of all must the proprietor or manager fish or admit to catching fish when his guests are not out. One evening I went out and had the good luck to get a fair seatrout of ten pounds. It was too good a fish to hide, so I decided to show it, maybe more with self-pride or conceit than with a view to offering some encouragement to others. I knew one guest might be upset, as I had arranged for him to fish beat one (the best) next day, and it was on this beat I had caught the fish. He was a poor fisher, and I decided to avoid all risk of strife and said I had caught it on beat four. All went well until mid-afternoon next day when my irate guest returned, having caught nothing. Why had I sent him to beat one when I went to beat four myself! That was my final evening's fishing from the hotel, so far as anyone knew; but it was strange how they did know. I have gone out after dinner, dressed in kilt, all very tidy and without sign of rod or tackle — to return two hours later, equally ship-shape, to be greeted with enquiry about what I had caught — and not be able to bring in my catch until everyone had gone to bed!

Most hotels, like ours, could not survive on anglers alone. The non-fisher was very important too. It is so today in nearly all angling inns, and the needs of the keen angler cannot be met without a huge increase in tariffs. The higher the tariffs, the greater the demands: rentals of fishings rise; the number of rods per beat increases, with less sport for each as time goes by. Perhaps the majority of anglers would prefer it this way but, selfish as it surely is, the old-time fisher does not relish it.

It is an education to meet and join ghillies and locals in the public bar and listen to all the news and rumours of local goings on. Strange things happened. One party of roadmen, billeted three miles from the taproom, found the road roller a good means of transport!

An old gamekeeper, a deafish worthy who lived alone seven miles up the lonely glen to the North, often got pulled into the river, bicycle and all, by a light shining from it and always too strong and bright for him on a Saturday night! At his funeral, ten miles back over the hills, he had many pall bearers for the long carry and much whisky was taken. At one halt a faithful mourner had another good dram, then thrust forward the bottle to the coffin — 'Have a drink, you old b . . .'. Not a move or a sound in reply. 'My God, he MUST be dead'! He was settled in his last resting place and all returned safely, but many tales of that trip to Groban and of old Fergie were told in that bar.

The answer may lie in chalets and self-catering units where day and night fishing can go on. There would seem to be plenty of open spaces and trout lochs for such in the Highlands, without any encroachment on the beauties of the land. But it is not so with salmon fishing: there is not much of it to be found and it must be treasured, not in its sterling value but in its sporting quality, which is so much more valuable and must be preserved.

Some hotels let useless water and have a stream of dissatisfied clients, but the good ones give a true assessment to enquirers and there are many of these. Try to find them. It's your money and your holiday. And there is no shortage of places where a non-fishing wife can be as comfortable and happy as her angler husband. A fishing hotel lounge can be most entertaining for the non-angler.

One hotel we stayed in abroad came near to my ideal. A good cold table was always available and the rod-room, drying-room and fish storage facilities were excellent. Alas, the beds were hard, the rooms sparsely furnished, and the hotel, by National law, unlicensed. The fishing arrangements were carelessly made — maybe even misleadingly — and not what I had so earnestly tried to arrange long in advance. And it was not cheap. During my two years' sojourn in Iceland I did not have opportunity to test the hotels, but the fishing was wonderful — albeit for brown trout and char only.

A modest reputation in angling and casting circles was a great help in my own hotel career, but all who came into the hotel did not know me. For years I had great fun with some of the bar-room experts. As I became older it became a great strain to listen to so much line-shooting. One evening I returned to a busy front hall after assisting in measuring out the distance markers for a casting competition which was to be held next day. An 'expert' asked me the distances and roared with laughter when I said up to sixty yards. All right for us up here, but the good casters could reach one hundred and fifty yards — yes, with a salmon fly. I knew better. He later flung a 'Field' to me with a report giving some casting results. Sure enough, 'One hundred and fifty yards'. But that was the aggregate of three casts! Next day, with a tingle of revenge in my blood, I had him called up to the casting platform through the public address system for all to see him perform. He had the line round his neck in no time but, stout politician that he was, he seemed undaunted though, perhaps, wiser. I cast well beyond sixty yards!

Hours were long, and the years began to take their toll, so I kept out of discussions latterly and took up golf. It was such a change to talk lightly of the lengths of putts rather than of fish and casts!

15

A Caster's Angle

In 1864 John Younger wrote in his book, River Angling for Salmon and Trout': 'The greatest requisite in an angler is the art of throwing his line properly' and, twelve years later, casting was referred to by Cotton. I quoted this in my paperback, 'The Art of Seatrout Fishing , now out of print, but I do not hesitate to repeat it here: 'The length of your line, to a man who knows how to handle his rod and to cast it, is no manner of encumbrance — and the length of the line is a mighty advantage to the fishing at a distance; and to fish fine and far off is first and principal for trout angling'. He could have included seatrout and salmon angling in this.

The ability to cast a long line is of great value. I could do so from early boyhood and seemed to have a gift for near perfect timing in my casting. It looks easy and effortless, even lazy, but there is no way in which I can cast farther without applying more force. The rhythm, timing and smoothness of action of an expert caster are essential to get the maximum distance and the greatest accuracy from any tackle, fly or bait. Except in a few cases, strength does not make up for casting faults. I found it disappointing to see the poor styles of so many of the world's great casters. The finest I have had the pleasure of watching was my friend, the late Pierre Creusevaut — a fine fisherman too. The athletic styles, or maybe it was showmanship, of many Europeans and Americans, did not fit into my picture of a fishing scene. I was primarily interested in tackle which could be used for fishing and not in the highly specialised outfits used in many casting events: this is a game — valuable for experiment in the development of tackle.

I was forty-two before I even heard of Tournament Casting. It was true, I won all the local amateur casting competitions I entered, and had not met anyone I could not outcast with trout or salmon tackle. At five feet eight inches in height, weighing ten stone two pounds, and with an army disability pension, my strength was rather limited.

A chance meeting in the cocktail bar led to a meeting with the late Captain T. L. (Tommy) Edwards. He cast out twice to show me how: truly I did not know what I was supposed to do until I saw him. He handed me the rod with what seemed to me a suspicion of disdain in his look. I took it and, with the line shooting out to click the reel, my first cast went over fifty yards. Tommy's hand went to his forehead as he flopped back on a rock with a 'C . . A . .' comment! Thereafter he showed me the tackle set-up, and Hardy's loaned it to me. But this did not teach me to cast: my father did that many years before.

Perhaps I was a natural caster but, even so, it took much practice and a lot of time and thought for me to attain my maximum distances and accuracy. But I won many open competitions in a brief spell. It is not easy to work all day, travel by car all night and compete next day well enough to win against those with carefully controlled physical exertions designed to produce an optimum performance. My determination to prove that a good fisherman could cast as well as any other in these Isles drove me on. I have yet to see a tournament caster from South of the Border demonstrate the reverse on our Scottish waters — and I have seen quite a few of the greatest try. I suppose this is understandable, in our different environments.

This brings to mind the end of one of those days when I surprised them. I offered to explain the reasons for this to one of them. He was delighted and we went to the river. I pointed out the spot where a fish would rise. My dropper came over, and up came the fish. I pulled the fly away intentionally. He could hardly speak from astonishment and excitement. His amazed look when I said I would rise it again and catch it was incredulous. I did just that. Back at the hotel two of the experts, with nods of approval from others, made it loud and clear that they thought us b . . liars. I was disappointed about that. I had thought great men were magnanimous — some were suddenly not so great!

Some anglers who were interested, and whom I helped with their casting, won Scottish titles. George Mackay of Lochinver won British titles, including a record, proving the casting potential of some fishermen. The conditions of fishing are usually difficult and this develops casting techniques which show up well on a casting platform. I regularly cast much further in practice, and hit more targets, than I ever did in competitions.

My first entry for a British Casting title was on a foul windy day. The water was in flood and flowing back, to tangle my shooting line under the platform after the first cast. It happened while I waited for the go-ahead to retrieve the fly — a quite unnecessary delay, but I did not question it. It was a disappointment, because I usually cast much further, and the fankle left me with little casting time. I had to be content with what I had done — an extension of the previous record by twelve yards! It was difficult not to let the fly touch the water behind, on the back cast. If the wind did help, which is questionable, it was there to help all others too. Almost immediately thereafter I ran into ways I was unaccustomed to meet — designed perhaps to keep me in check. Thereafter I decided to go my own way. I did so and won many other events, including the British Victor Ludorum — with ten second places in the fourteen events! In each event one is up against a specialist in that event. In the following years I specialised too, and won the events! I gave it all up after three or four years: I was content. I know several fishermen who could outcast most tournament casters I have seen, with little effort. The British Casting Association is a small affair, with a minute number of casters in proportion to the number of anglers who are not attracted to these competitions. The mystery puts them off. But it need not: there is none!

Enough of that; there is another side to it all.

When I was young, success more often than not depended on casting a long line, to reach lies which had not been reached earlier in the day, and disturbed or denuded of fish. I learned how great and how vital is the difference between casting a fly a long distance and fishing a fly at a long distance. I broke many rods too, not by standing on them or sticking the point into the ground ahead, but by casting. I am sure they were not built to stand the power I applied at the critical stage of my cast; perhaps the lines were too heavy. On reflection I know I asked too much of them — a fault not in my technique, but in failure to assess this critical stress. At any rate, I like to think so.

There are lies in rivers which can be reached by many anglers but not fished properly — with a short rod or a long one. A different stance and a long line allows the good caster to fish them as he should. I fish a short line — as short as the average angler — and he is a very poor caster technically. I learned early in life that casting a long line when only a short one is needed is just as useless or wrong as the reverse. Knowledge and experience are needed to know where the fish lie, and it is the fisher who can reach it, and have the fly fish the lie, who catches the fish — be they by the far bank or the near one.

Many good anglers are content with their styles and will not make an effort to improve their casting. They try to shrug off the advantages of good casting by arguing that they catch as many fish as the next man. I will not argue. Sometimes they do and, often they do, because the next man is invariably an equally poor caster of a fly. The spinner with the fixed spool reel is an excellent caster — a fishing standard easy to reach.

It is a pity there are so few casting competitions and so few demonstrations given by experts. Better casting does lead to better fishing. Do not, however, become obsessed by a drive to cast a long line. Great distances need not be cast, and an angler need not fear being belittled if his performance does not measure up to that of some of the top casters. I have seen a number of well-known anglers brought down to reality: what seems a long cast when fishing, is often not so when measured from the casting point to where the fly lands. Thirty yards is a very long cast, and anglers, like golfers, may exaggerate sometimes. I would not destroy this dream world completely, but a little reality is necessary sometimes! And the technique in correct casting is the same for everyone, whether for the capture of fish or the breaking of casting records.

I get great pleasure out of the proper execution of any particular cast. One's casting can be improved very easily but it is not so with fishing ability — this grows only with experience. Freedom from casting worries allows for greater concentration on the presentation of the fly or bait. The trees and bushes, or a wind, do not present too serious problems to the able caster, yet they may prove so troublesome to the poor one that he has to give up. There is no need to cast a long line all the time, but to be able to do so when necessary is no burden to bear and may well add to the weight of fish to be carried home.

Good casting can make fishing easy; but tackle designed specially to make casting easy may make the fishing of the flies extremely difficult. Using a heavy line with a fine cast may be right for casting a long distance, but it is not good for fishing. I was lucky enough with my fishing to have a reputation as a good angler thrust upon me in various parts of the country and, indeed, abroad. I ventured into tournament casting and succeeded in becoming associated with it. The result was I had to listen to talk of how tournament casters can cast but not fish, and much other nonsense about the tackle used at these tournaments. I prefer my old status of good angler but, following my sojourn in tournament casting circles, I cannot do other than give credit to the tournament caster.

Casting is a considerable part of fishing, and tournament casters can undoubtedly cast well with at least one type of rod, though many excel with a variety of outfits. Some I have seen have not had the opportunity to fish widely or to gain experience by fishing months on end each year. Some are average fishermen, some are fine anglers. But I believe that the finest fishermen I have known would have been at the top in the tournament world had they entered it.

Finally, when you have the opportunity, go and watch an expert. You will enjoy the sight and learn from it — and your fishing will benefit.

Index

Alevins   5, 6
Amboise   33
Arousing fish   15
Ashley Cooper   19

'Backing' a pool   14
Baggit (Baggot)   2
Ballantyne, Mrs G. W.   8
Banks   29, 30
Barbara   33, 70
Beaching   54
Best Catch   18
Black Doctor   75
Bogie Roll   46
Botulism   86
Boulder   13, 26
Breeze   22
British Casting Assoc.   93
Brooks, Joe   77

Canada   15
Carbon Fibre   77
Caster's Angle   91 to 95
Casting   12 to 14, 17, 18, 32,
                           77, 89, 94
Chalmers   76
Char   30, 31
Coho Salmon   56
Colour   75
Concentration   27

Cotton   91
Courtesy   71 to 74
Creusevaut, Pierre   33, 91
Crosby, Bing   78

Dapping   21
Derwent   78
Dibbling   19, 21
Disturbance   14, 22, 27, 30,
                   31, 52, 55 to 59, 68,
                   70, 72, 73, 76, 87, 93
Dog days   26
Drift   72
Drive   9, 69
Dropper   18, 19, 21, 22, 23,
                       25, 33, 76, 92
Drought   15

Edwards, T.   92
Ewe   53

Farlow   18, 33
Faroes   6
Fergie   88
Finnock   25
Flasher   15
Flip   12, 13
Fly   9 to 14, 16, 17, 23, 25,
                       27, 37, 75
Foul-hooked   20, 41, 69

Francis Francis 76
Fry 5, 6, 80, 81

Gaffing 49 to 54
Gairbhe river 53, 82
Garry river 79
Geared reel 47
Ghillie 10, 14, 18, 19, 27, 30, 31, 33, 34, 50, 58, 61 to 66, 79, 81, 88
Green Highlander 75
Greenland 6, 82
Grilse 6, 7, 21, 35, 49, 54
Grimersta 58
Groban 88

Hancock, Mr G. M. 19
Handlining 13, 14, 34, 36, 37, 42, 47, 52, 76
Hanging the fly 12, 23
Hardy 92
Harling 67
Hooks 36
Hope 75
Hotels 85 to 89
Hurrying the fly 23, 36
Hydro 80

Ice 10, 14
Iceland 89
Intuition 75 to 78

Jock Scott 17, 25, 75
Johansen, Johan 70
Jumping fish 22

Kelts 50
Kipper 86
Kirkaig 25, 37, 44

Labrador 15
Ladder Pool 43
Large salmon 8, 44

Leader thickness 21
Lies 13, 23, 24, 29, 30, 37, 47, 56, 57, 62, 72, 73, 93
Life (in the fly) 13
Light 10, 16, 24, 26, 27, 28
Line go 35
Lines 11, 12, 16, 17, 18, 21, 22, 34, 36, 38, 76, 77, 95
Low water 24

Mackay, George 92

Maree, Loch 64, 82
Mendelssohn 85
Mending the line 13, 23, 25
Morrel, Mr 32
My first salmon 16, 17

Netting 49 to 54, 80, 81, 82
Norway 1, 6, 9, 69, 78

Otter 7
Otter board effect 43, 58
Ova 2, 5, 6, 82

Pain 41, 42, 43
Paris 33
Parr 2, 5, 6, 68
Parr-tail 68
Persuasion 43
Peter Ross 25, 32
Pezon et Michel 33
Playing a fish 25, 41 to 48
Poaching 30, 82
Poker 68
Polaroids 26, 27, 37, 58
Prawn 15, 68, 69
Progress 12, 14
Pumping 45, 46, 52

Rawner 2
Redds 1, 4, 5, 6, 81
Reel 37, 42, 45, 47, 52

Reflex Action 7, 15, 37
Rises 33, 35 to 39, 42, 86
Ritz, Charles 33
Rods 11, 13, 17, 18, 25, 26,
34, 39, 41, 47, 77, 93
Rowan gatherers 2
Running fish 15, 30

Salmon 1 to 8
Salmon in lochs 29 to 34
Salmon in rivers 9 to 28
Salmo — salar 1
Seals 7
Seatrout 20, 31, 32, 33, 49,
82, 87, 91
Second return 6
Shade 24
Sharpe 77
Shooting a line 18, 77
'Short' rise 21, 34, 76
Short rod 24, 25, 34, 45, 56,
59, 76, 77
Silver Doctor 27
Smolts 6, 7, 80
Sna' bree 10
Snow 10, 11, 14, 26
Spey 78
Spinner 9, 15, 67 to 70, 94

Strike 33, 35, 36, 37, 38, 39
Sulking 43
Switching 13

Tailing 6, 33, 49 to 54
Taking times 13, 14
Television 78
Temperature 12, 14, 16, 31, 38
Three flies 19, 20, 21, 22, 32, 54
Touch 13
Tournament caster 63
Trolling 15, 58, 67, 68, 70
Tummel Bridge 79, 85
Twelve footer 18
Two at once 21

U.D.N. 80, 81, 82
Unbalanced tackle 19

Wading 22, 42, 50, 55,
56, 62, 72
Wading stick 56
Walking 45, 46, 52
Water bailiffs 72
Wee sma' 'oors 87
Worm 67, 68, 69

Younger, John 91